▪ THE PISAN CANTOS ▪

ALSO BY EZRA POUND

ABC of Reading

The Cantos

The Classic Noh Theatre of Japan

Collected Early Poems, edited by Michael John King

Confucius, trans.

Confucius to Cummings, edited with Marcella Spann

The Correspondence of Ezra Pound

Pound/Ford, edited by Brita Lindberg-Seyersted

Pound/Joyce, edited by Forrest Read

Pound/Lewis, edited by Timothy Materer

Pound/The Little Review, edited by Thomas L. Scott,
Melvin J. Friedman, and Jackson R. Bryer

Pound/Williams, edited by Hugh Witemeyer

Pound/Zukofsky, edited by Barry Ahearn

Dyptich: Rome–London

A Draft of XXX Cantos

Sophokles' *Elektra*, trans. with Rudd Fleming

Ezra Pound and the Visual Arts, edited by Harriet Zinnes

Gaudier-Brzeska

Guide to Kulchur

Literary Essays, edited by T.S. Eliot

Pavannes and Divagations

Personae

Selected Cantos

Selected Letters: 1907–1941, edited by D.D. Paige

Selected Poems

Selected Prose 1909–1965, edited by William Cookson

The Spirit of Romance

Translations

A Walking Tour in Southern France, edited by Richard Sieburth

Sophokles' *Women of Trachis*, trans.

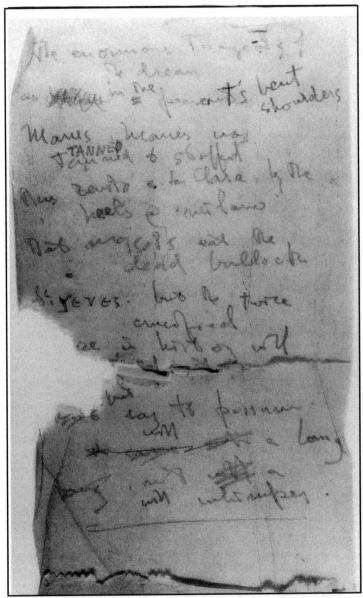

The sheets of toilet paper on which Pound wrote the revised
opening of *The Pisan Cantos*

EZRA POUND
THE PISAN CANTOS

EDITED AND ANNOTATED
WITH AN INTRODUCTION
BY RICHARD SIEBURTH

A NEW DIRECTIONS BOOK

Frontispiece reproduced from a facsimile, in the James Laughlin Collection, of the lost original; courtesy of Leila Laughlin Javitch and Daniel Javitch.

Book design by Sylvia Frezzolini Severance
Manufactured in the United States of America
New Directions Books are printed on acid-free paper.
First published as New Directions Paperbook 970 in 2003
Published simultaneously in Canada by Penguin Books Canada Limited

Library of Congress Cataloging-in-Publication Data
Pound, Ezra, 1885–1972.
    The Pisan cantos / Ezra Pound ; edited and annotated with an introduction by Richard Sieburth.
        p.   cm.—(New DIrections paperbook ; 970)
Includes bibliographical references and index.
    ISBN: 0-8112-1558-X (pbk. : alk. paper)
    1. Sieburth, Richard. II. Title.
PS3531.082P5 2003
811'.52—dc22

                                                        2003014114

New Directions Books are published for James Laughlin
by New Directions Publishing Corporation,
80 Eighth Avenue, New York, NY 10011

CONTENTS

INTRODUCTION

On April 28, 1945, while attempting to flee to Switzerland in a convoy of retreating German soldiers, Benito Mussolini and his mistress Clara Patacci were captured and summarily shot to death by Italian partisans in the small village of Dongo, not far from Lake Como. Under cover of night, their bodies were trucked to Milan and, in memory of fifteen anti-Fascists who had recently been executed in that very square, dumped in the Piazzale Loreto, where they were kicked and spat upon by an angry crowd. In an image reproduced by newspapers throughout the world, the corpses were then hoisted onto an improvised scaffold and strung up by their heels, Il Duce in undershirt with his boots still on, his mistress with her skirt hiked to her thighs and midriff fully exposed—an appropriately theatrical end to the Era Fascista, tersely memorialized in the opening lines of *The Pisan Cantos*: "Thus Ben and la Clara *a Milano* / by the heels at Milano . . ."

Several days later, on the morning of May 3, as he sat alone at his desk translating Mencius in Sant'Ambrogio among the quiet hills above Rapallo, Ezra Pound, American expatriate and known Fascist sympathizer, was interrupted by two men with tommy guns who identified themselves as partisans. Both his wife, Dorothy, and his companion, Olga Rudge—whom wartime circumstances had thrown into a strained menage-à-trois in this small hillside cottage—were away on errands. Fearing for his life, Pound had little choice but to follow his captors and, before locking up the house, hastily slipped a copy of the Confucian Classics and a small Chinese dictionary into his pockets. On the way down the hill path, he picked up a eucalyptus seed to carry with him as a memento on a journey whose precise destination—immediate death by firing squad? repatriation to the United States?—lay, for the moment, entirely in the dark. "Eucalyptus that is for memory," he later observed in Canto 74. During his three months of subsequent captivity in a U.S. military prison camp near Pisa, this mnemonic eucalyptus "nib" with its "cat-faced" markings was never far from the poet's side—his secret talisman to guard against the oblivion of Circe's pig-sty.[1]

The men with the tommy guns escorted him to a command post at Zoagli, just to the south of Rapallo, where Olga Rudge finally managed to catch up with him. The two were then taken to *partigiani* headquarters in Chiarvari, with Pound later recalling that at the sight of the walls stained with the blood of recent executions, he thought he was "finished there and then." The local commander, however, having no particular warrant for his arrest, allowed him to make his way to nearby Lavagna to give himself up to the American military authorities—who, when it became clear that they had a rather unusual prisoner in their custody, in turn decided to pass the buck. Pound and his companion were accordingly transferred by jeep to U.S. Counter Intelligence Corps headquarters in Genoa, where they waited until the following day for the arrival of Major Frank L. Amprim, the FBI special agent assigned by J. Edgar Hoover to gather evidence pertinent to the Justice Department's 1943 federal grand jury indictment of the poet on charges of treason for his wartime activities as a broadcaster on Radio Rome.

All told, Pound spent three weeks at the CIC headquarters. Olga was driven back to Sant'Ambrogio on May 7, later describing her four days in Genoa—with her man finally all to herself and ample food for the two of them—as "among the happiest of my life." Now that he was safely in American hands, Pound's own mood was no less ebullient. His first request to Amprin when the formal questioning began on the morning of May 5 was permission to send a cable addressed to President Truman in which he offered personally to negotiate a "just peace" with Japan, given his familiarity with work of American Orientalist Ernest Fenollosa and his previous contacts with the Japanese embassy in Italy. The cable was never sent (much to Pound's indignation), nor was he, as he subsequently demanded, given access to the airwaves to read the script of a final radio broadcast he had especially prepared for the occasion. Entitled "Ashes of Europe Calling," it presented in telegraphic fashion his recommendations for postwar foreign policy: American management of Italy until new elections, leniency toward Germany, the establishment of a state in Palestine as "national home & symbol of jewry," and peace with Japan. It concluded with this bit of advice for America: "In the mean time there is Europe, to win or lose." The material was duly forwarded on to J. Edgar Hoover.

Over the next two days, Amprim and his commanding officer, Ramon Arrizabalaga, interrogated Pound at length, eliciting a six-page "Sworn Statement" in which their prisoner chronicled the milestones of his existence— his birth in Hailey, Idaho, in 1885, his move to London in 1908, followed by his 1920–24 sojourn in Paris and his subsequent residence in Rapallo, where he had become increasingly drawn to the what he called the "New Deal" that Mussolini was effecting in Fascist Italy. Most of the affidavit, however, was devoted to a detailed description of the accused's activities between 1940 and 1943 as a broadcaster for Radio Rome. As Pound explained, he generally wrote his ten- to fifteen-minute speeches (roughly 120 in all, for which he received approximately $18 each) at his home in Rapallo, then traveled to the studio of the EIAR (Ente Italiana Audizione Radio) in Rome to record them on discs in batches of ten to twenty for subsequent shortwave broadcast—some of them so incoherent that Italian officials suspected he might be a double agent communicating in secret code. Although harshly critical of the economic and foreign policies of the United States and filled with scurrilous diatribes against Roosevelt and his gang of Jewish financiers, these speeches—at least to Pound's mind—did not constitute treasonable offenses per se. True, he had erred gravely by returning to the microphone after war had been declared on December 7, 1941 ("I hope the errors will be considered in relation to the main picture"), but by campaigning against U.S. involvement in a foreign war he had merely been "making a test case for the freedom of speech," especially given the fact that he had been offered a guarantee by the Italian authorities, read at the beginning of each broadcast, "that I should *not* be asked to say anything contrary to my own conscience or contrary to my duties as an American citizen."

Confident that he had fully explained and exonerated himself—the virulently anti-Semitic tenor of his broadcasts, morally unconscionable but technically not treasonable, was passed over in silence by all parties—Pound appended in his defense two further documents outlining the "main foundations of my beliefs and the objects of my thirty years of writing." These included: a brief history of the malfeasances of the European and American banking systems; passing praise for Lenin's critique of capitalism (with Pound expressing hopes that he might learn Georgian in order to confer with Stalin about monetary reform); a précis of Confucian doctrine as set forth in *The Great Learning*; a bibliography for further reading (among which, the collected works of John Adams and Thomas Jefferson); a discussion of the U.S. government's betrayal of the "money clause" in the Constitution; and further offers to act as a diplomatic go-between with Japan ("if I could bring the slaughter in the Pacific to a sane and speedy end, I should, I believe, have justified my existence").

On May 8, the day Germany unconditionally surrendered, Pound was interviewed in Genoa by a reporter representing the *Philadelphia Record* and the *Chicago Sun*. Exhibiting his usual talkative penchant for shooting himself in the foot, the fifty-nine-year-old poet called Adolf Hitler "a Jeanne d'Arc, a saint" (adding, "like many martyrs, he held extreme views") and described Mussolini as "a very human, imperfect character who lost his head"—an attempt, perhaps, to distance himself from his previous allegiances, but certainly not likely to play well on the wire services back home. But encouraged as he was by the affable atmosphere of the first few days of interrogation, his old Dada bravado remained intact, for he informed the reporter: "If I am not shot for treason, I think my chances of seeing Truman are good." Persuaded that with Amprim's assistance he had now prepared an airtight defense should his case actually come to trial,

Pound spent the next two weeks at Genoa in what Olga Rudge described to T.S. Eliot as a state of "Confucian serenity"—well fed, decently lodged, free from domestic tensions, and finally at leisure to resume his all-important English translation of *The Great Learning*, which contained the ancient Chinese "blueprint" for the reconstruction of "civilization" out of the rubble of Europe.

Amprim, in whose sympathy and meticulousness Pound placed absolute trust, was meanwhile directing agents in Rome and making his own visits to Sant'Ambrogio to gather incriminating evidence: the poet's typewriter, an Everest portable with a misaligned "t," various pencils, a black (Swan) fountain pen, and nearly 7,000 pages of documents—letters, articles, broadcast scripts—that would later fill fourteen volumes of FBI files. Though the evidence (much of it illegally obtained without search warrants) against Pound was mounting, the Justice Department still lacked the key element for its case, namely, the testimony of at least two witnesses to each overt act of treason, as mandated by the U.S. Constitution. Until such witnesses could be produced, Pound was to remain in custody in Italy. On May 22, the CIC in Genoa received the following cable from Washington:

> American Civilian Doctor EZRA LOOMIS POUND reference
> Fifth Army cable 2006 under federal grand jury indictment for
> treason.
> Transfer without delay under guard to MTOUSA [Mediterranean
> Theatre of Operations, USA] Disciplinary Training Center for con-
> finement pending disposition instructions. Exercise utmost security
> measures to prevent escape or suicide. No press interviews authorized.
> Accord no preferential treatment.

Two days later, several jeeploads of military police arrived to escort the prisoner down the coast to Pisa. Unceremoniously relieved of his shoestrings, belt, and necktie, and handcuffed to a huge MP for transport, Pound was incredulous: "I don't understand it," he said to Arrizabalga. "Do they know who I am?" The latter merely replied: "Yes they do, Mr. Pound."

◆ ◆ ◆

The U.S. Army's Disciplinary Training Center (DTC), situated on a dusty one-half-mile-square tract near the village of Metato just to the north of Pisa, housed some 3,600 military prisoners—mostly African-American and guilty of such offenses as going AWOL (22%), desertion (15%), misbehavior before the enemy, murder, rape, or larceny (7%), and disobedience (5%). Conceived (like

Dante's Purgatory) as a "reprogramming" or "rehabilitation" facility, the DTC offered its "trainees" the opportunity of working off their full sentences by enduring fourteen hours a day of harshly regimented tasks and forced drills. After an appropriate period of penance (usually eight to fourteen months), prisoners were awarded clemency and, in a weekly Saturday ceremony on the parade grounds, "graduated" as full-fledged privates, ready to be returned to active service. Pound was the only civilian inmate in the camp and, in the temporary absence of its commander, Lieutenant Colonel John L. Steele, overzealous subordinates, no doubt awed by the Washington cable's warnings about escape or suicide, had decided to confine their dangerous war criminal in one of the camp's "death cells"—a six-by-six-foot steel cage, open to the elements, which had been specially reinforced the night before Pound's arrival with sections of heavy "airstrip" steel mesh normally used to lay down temporary runways.

Washington had stipulated that the prisoner be accorded no preferential treatment. Orders were therefore given that he be held completely incommunicado: isolated in his cell under the constant observation of a special guard, with the Mediterranean sun beating down on him all day and floodlights trained on him all night, his eyes badly inflamed by all the dust and glare, he was allowed no exercise privileges, no bed, no belt, no shoelaces, and above all, no verbal contact with the world around him—except for daily conversations with the camp's Roman Catholic chaplain.[2] Still under the impression that he was merely being temporarily detained at the DTC until air transport could be arranged to fly him back to Washington (whether to "straighten out" Truman or stand trial), trainee Pound initially held up fairly well under the circumstances. Witnesses at the DTC later remembered him as reading his Confucius for hours on end, contemplating the surrounding landscape, engaging in shadow boxing, fencing, and imaginary tennis matches in his cage, and ingeniously arranging the tiny pup tent which, out of sheer mercy, had eventually been issued to him to protect him from the wind and sun and rain of the Pisan plain.

But after some two and a half weeks of this, the prisoner foundered. The breakdown is discreetly recorded in Canto 80, with its author indirectly comparing his plight to that of Odysseus, violently tossed from his raft by the rage of Poseidon and only saved from drowning through the intercession of the white sea goddess Leucothea:

> hast'ou swum in a sea of air strip
>> through an aeon of nothingness,
> when the raft broke and the waters went over me
>>> (80.665–67)*

* References to The Pisan Cantos are givien by Canto number, followed by line numbers.

Rescue in this case came not from the goddess (though avatars of her divine compassion are everywhere present in The Pisan Cantos), but from the DTC medical staff who, warned by the guards of the prisoner's deteriorating condition, decided to remove him from his solitary death cell. A few days later, on June 14 and 15, having spent three weeks in the "gorilla cage" (as he called it), Pound was examined by two camp psychiatrists. The first reported that the prisoner claimed to have undergone a "spell" the previous week while sitting in the sun and that he was "having difficulty in concentration." He added: "Patient states that he has been confined in a rather small space [and] has become afraid of the door and the lock of his enclosure. Also states he worries a great deal that he'll forget some messages which he wishes eventually to tell others." The second psychiatrist, similarly registering the patient's complaints of "temporary periods of confusion, anxiety, feelings of frustration, and excessive fatigability," concluded with the recommendation that "due to his age and loss of personality resilience, prolonged exposure in present environment may precipitate a mental breakdown, of which premonitory symptoms are discernible. Early transfer to the United States or to an institution in this theatre with more adequate facilities for care is recommended." As a result, the prisoner was now officially moved to his own private tent in the medical compound.

Both army psychiatrists had been careful to point out that the patient, while exhibiting symptoms of extreme stress, was in no way mentally deranged: he displayed "no paranoia, delusions nor hallucinations," and there was "no evidence of psychosis, neurosis or psychopathy." Pound's own subsequent accounts of what befell him in the cage paint a more extreme picture of the trauma—or, as he termed it, the "lesion"—he had undergone. He later reported to various psychiatrists at St. Elizabeths Hospital in Washington, D.C., that he had "burst a mainspring" at Pisa—a condition, he further informed his lawyer, Julian Cornell, that had caused him "violent terror and hysteria" and that had resulted in "a complete loss of memory." Whether Pound's repeated insistence on the "amnesia" he had experienced in the cage was merely a ploy to buttress his plea of insanity when facing trial for treason later that fall of course remains open to question. But as far as the composition of The Pisan Cantos is concerned, this myth of an originary trauma, be it the violent collapse of Mussolini's Italy or that of the poet's own mind, is vital to an understanding of how the poem stages its theater of memory—and of forgetting.

Now installed in his own officer's tent—pyramidal in shape, with a smoke-hole at the top through which the ascent of butterflies and the processions of constellations could be glimpsed—the prisoner proceeded to regather his scattered wits, gratefully regaining terra firma ("so kissed the earth after sleeping on concrete," 77.171). A daily regimen of exercise was soon established. As Robert Allen, a member of the DTC medical staff, later recalled: "He found an old broom handle that became a tennis racket, a billiard cue, a rapier, a baseball bat to hit small stones and a stick which he swung out smartly to match his long stride. His constitutionals wore a circular path in the compound grass." Still forbidden any contact with his fellow prisoners, he would report on special sick call in the evening to receive drops for his inflamed eyes—and with his vision now beginning to heal, he seemed to rediscover his former garrulity after three weeks of enforced muteness, lecturing camp commander Lieutenant Colonel Steele on the true nature of money and launching into jeremiads against "the dunghill usurers" for the edification of the medical orderlies, eyes flashing with prophetic wrath.

By late June or early July, Pound had sufficiently recovered to resume work on the Cantos—his as-of-yet unfinished Odyssean epic "including history," nearly thirty years in the making but which, given his current plight at the DTC, would now take an unexpectedly elegiac and autobiographical turn in Cantos 74 through 84, later published in 1948 under the title The Pisan Cantos and considered by most critics as the finest section of Pound's magnum opus. The first portion of his epic had appeared in Paris in 1925 under the title of A Draft of XVI Cantos of Ezra Pound for the Beginning of a Poem of some Length. This was followed by A Draft of XXX Cantos in 1930, Eleven New Cantos XXI–XLI in 1934, and The Fifth Decad of Cantos in 1937. Loosely following the scheme of Dante's Divine Comedy, the most recent installment of his sprawling work-in-progress, Cantos LII–LXXI, published in 1940 to mixed reviews, had advanced the poem out of its Inferno (peopled by historical figures merely "dominated by human emotions") and through what Pound called "the Purgatory of human error." Juxtaposing a swift conspectus of three millennia of Chinese history (lifted from De Mailla's eighteenth-century Histoire générale de la Chine) with a cubist collage of the Works and Days of John Adams, paterfamilias of a great Confucian American dynasty, Cantos LII–LXXI didactically illustrated the Enlightenment virtues of "constructive effort" while providing a transcultural narrative of men "putting order into things" and thus (presumably like Il Duce) preparing the advent of paradise on earth.

By 1940, Pound was therefore fairly confident that he would need only one more volume to wrap his poem up. As he wrote George Santayana: "I have . . . got to the end of a job or part of a job (money in history) and for personal ends have got to tackle philosophy for my 'paradise'"—the philosophy in question involving an idiosyncratic amalgam of Confucius (for his ethics) and the neo-Platonist Duns Scotus Erigena (for his "light philosophy"). But in this case, as in so many others, history would prove Pound grievously wrong. Instead of tracing a luminous ascent toward a Paradiso of benevolence, the poet's wartime radio broadcasts dramatized a sensibility gone to hell, mired in the *contrappasso* of its own manic hatreds. Splinters of paradise appeared in some of Pound's (mostly manuscript) poetic fragments of the '40s, but the succeeding two Cantos, composed in late 1944 and subsequently published in a minor naval newspaper of the Salò Republic—and withheld from complete editions of the *Cantos* until 1985—veered back into the wrathful underworld of Italian Fascism. In Canto 72, the aged shade of the futurist Filippo Tommaso Marinetti materializes to the poet, demanding rebirth and rejuvenation so that he might rejoin the Axis forces in their heroic last-ditch stand against the encroaching Allied armies. In Canto 73, the spirit of Guido Cavalcanti in turn appears to sing the praises of a Romagnole girl who, in revenge for her rape by Allied soldiers, leads an unwitting troop of Canadians to their deaths in a minefield, sacrificing herself in the process. Coming as they do from the author of some of the greatest antiwar poetry of his century (*Cathay, Hugh Selwyn Mauberley*), Cantos 72 and 73 mark the moral nadir of the poem.[3]

◆ ◆ ◆

Apart from the cracker-barrel "Murkn" dialect of his radio broadcasts, Pound wrote almost exclusively in Italian during the war. In addition to the two above-mentioned "Salò Cantos," he published some six original books and pamphlets in his adopted language between 1942 and 1944, as well as Italian translations of the Confucian *Great Digest* (*Testamento di Confucio*) and *Doctrine of the Mean*—whose Italian title, *L'Asse che non vacilla* [i.e. "The Unwavering Axis"] provoked the destruction of most of the edition as pro-Fascist propaganda after the Liberation. Even as he returned to the Paradiso section of his *Cantos* in January-February 1945, recording in draft form a series of private visionary encounters amid the olive groves and cliffs above Rapallo, Pound's poetic medium of choice remained Italian—as in this glimpse of the compassionate figure of Cunizza, located by Dante in the *terzo cielo*, the heaven of Love:

io la vidi
come Kuanina, col ramo di salce / vidi l'eterna
dolcezza formata: di misericorda la madre,
dei mar' protettrice / socorso in naufraggio / manifesto

[I saw her
as Kuanon, with willow branch / saw the eternal
sweetness created: of pity the mother,
protectress of the seas / succor in shipwreck / manifest]

As Ronald Bush has demonstrated, a direct line can be drawn between these first-person Dantescan epiphanies recorded in Pound's fragmentary Italian Cantos of early 1945 and the reapparition of the benevolent goddess figure at the very outset of the *The Pisan Cantos*, promising succor to the shipwrecked poet.[4] In its initial form, the entire Pisan sequence began under the sign of her forgiving maternal gaze (now line 12):

> The suave eyes, quiet, not scornful

—which, several pages later, modulates into her resurgence (as in the Italian drafts) in the guise of the Japanese bodhisattva of mercy (74.131) and eventually climaxes with her full disclosure as Aphrodite rising from the sea (74.341).

As he began composing his Cantos at the DTC, Pound therefore already had in mind the paradisal scenario he wanted to rehearse in this sequence of the poem: the erotico-mystical encounters of the wandering Odysseus-Dante-Pound with a series of goddesses whose radiant theophanies provide what in a 1927 letter he had described as "the 'magic moment' or moment of metamorphosis, bust thru from quotidian into 'divine or permanent world.'" As magic as they might be, however, these moments of goddess-induced transcendence may be the least convincing passages in *The Pisan Cantos*—less because of their Parnassian classical garb (the aerial Aphrodite and Diana balanced against the chthonic Gea and Kore) than because they somehow feel too programmatic, emerging as they do from Pound's preconceived plan for his Paradiso in the Italian drafts of early 1945. As Charles Olson, the *Cantos'* keenest disciple and critic, observed to Robert Creeley in 1950, when Pound writes of goddesses in the Pisans, "he goes literary." The passages where Pound truly "scored," Olson continued, were those in which the quotidian actualities of the stockade at Pisa seemed to be most casually and delicately notated ("that is such gentilities as rain, grass, bird on a wire, 5, now 3, Metechevsky or whatever, tents, the trillings, rather than the thrustings"). But above all, Olson concluded, "where the right is, is, that he goeth by language."[5]

That he goeth by language. When imprisoned at Pisa, Pound had not composed any significant verse in English for over five years. He had last visited the United States for a three-month stay in the spring of 1939, his first return since 1911—the entirety of his professional writing career having been spent abroad, diasporically removed (except for a brief parenthesis in Paris in the early '20s frequenting his fellow expatriates) from the daily textures of American speech. His initial three weeks of enforced silence in solitary confinement at the DTC therefore represented the first time in years that, after the hysterical logorrhea of his radio broadcasts, he was actually forced to shut up ("and so his mouth was removed," 74.74) and listen to the world around him, the snatches of overheard GI conversation in turn opening up the entire echo chamber of remembered voices into which the poet of the Pisans, like Odysseus in Hades, makes his descent:

> "If you had a f. . . .n' brain you'd be dangerous"
>   remarks Romano Ramona
>   to a by him designated c.s. in the scabies ward
>   the army vocabulary contains almost 48 words
> one verb and participle one substantive   ὕλη
>   one adjective and one phrase sexless that is
> used as a sort of pronoun
> from a watchman's club to a vamp or fair lady
>   (77.203–10)

This bit of ethnographic observation modulates, some twenty lines later, into Pound's memories of his encounters in pre-World War I Paris with two now-for-gotten figures: Henri-Martin Barzun, an avant-garde proponent of *simultanéiste* poetry (which involved the visual scoring on the page, or even phonographic recording, of several voices at once), and Jean Rousselot, a professor of experi-mental phonetics at the Collège de France who had devised a machine to meas-ure the sound waves emitted by the irregular meters of the new *vers libre*—thus contributing, so Pound believed, to the invention of sonar.

These two principles—namely, the "simultaneist" superimposition of voic-es and the fine-tuned registration of the variable prosodies of free verse ("To break the pentameter, that was the first heave," 81.55)—had shaped the tech-nique of Pound's epic from its inception, and their application may be observed in his celebrated editing of the manuscript of T. S. Eliot's *The Waste Land* (orig-inally entitled "He Do The Police In Different Voices"). What sets the poetry of the Pisans apart from the earlier Cantos, however, is its far greater alertness to the demotic cadences of American speech—and, as a corollary, to those of ver-nacular Italian, French, or British. As he sits confined to the solitary listening post of his cage or tent, Pound's ear for "the very language of men" (Wordsworth) begins to rival that of his old friend, William Carlos Williams:

> and the guards op/ of the. . .
>   was lower than that of the prisoners
>   "all the g.d. m.f. generals c.s. all of 'em fascists"

"fer a bag o' Dukes"
"the things I saye an' doo"
(74.398–400)

"St. Louis Till" as Green called him. Latin !
"I studied latin" said perhaps his smaller companion.
"Hey Snag, what's in the bibl' ?
what are the books of the bibl' ?
Name 'em! don't bullshit me!"
"Hobo Williams, the queen of them all"
"Hey / Crawford, come over here / "
(77.269–75)

or Whiteside:
"ah certainly dew lak dawgs
ah goin' tuh wash you"
(no, not to the author, to the canine unwilling in question)
(79.33–36)

The DTC was the only integrated command in the entire Mediterranean the-
ater and its prison population overwhelmingly African-American. Although the
Pisans open with an evocation of the immaculately bleached bones of the dead
Confucius ("what whiteness will you add to this whiteness,/what candor?"
74.17–18) and close with a visionary white-out reminiscent of the Romantic
Sublime ('Carrara/snow on the marble/snow-white/against stone white," 84.42–45),
the first Canto in the sequence instead goes on to portray the shock and disori-
entation of a prisoner who, like the protagonist of some traditional American
captivity narrative, has just been plunged into a world of blackness, experienc-
ing St. John of the Cross's dark night of the soul:

is it blacker? was it blacker? Núξ animae?
is there a blacker or was it merely San Juan with a belly ache
writing ad posteros
in short shall we look for a deeper or is this the bottom?
(74.449–52)

In this heart of darkness, with his fate and identity still uncertain, the prisoner
casts his lot not with the American military victors but with their victims, not
with the masters, but with their slaves.[6] Overhearing or half-glimpsing his

African-American "companions in misery" on daily sick call, he reimagines the horror of the Middle Passage:

> magna NOX animae with Barabbas and 2 thieves beside me,
>   the wards like a slave ship
>   Mr Edwards, Hudson, Henry *comes miseriae*
>   Comites Kernes, Green and Tom Wilson
>   God's messenger Whiteside
>   (74.393–97)

Which, several lines later, is rephrased as the bestialization of Odysseus and his crew on Circe's island (the Latin underscoring "I too in the pig-sty," seeing the "corpses of souls"):

>   ac ego in harum
> so lay men in Circe's swine-sty;
>   ivi in harum *ego* ac vidi cadaveres animae
>   "c'mon small fry" sd/ the little coon to the big black;
> of the slaver as seen between decks
>   and all the presidents
> Washington Adams Monroe Polk Tyler
>   (74.403–9)

The roll call of names in this passage (such lists of the living dead occur as a leitmotif throughout the Pisans, in homage to Homer's catalogues) is explained in a brief and typically double-edged note Pound wrote to the "Base Censor" when he finally sent out his manuscript to his wife for retyping:

> The form of the poem and main progress is conditioned by its own inner shape, but the life of the D.T.C. passing OUTSIDE the scheme cannot but impinge, or break into the main flow. The proper names given are mostly those of men of sick call seen passing my tent. A very brief allusion to further study in names, that is, I am interested to note the prevalence of early American names, either of whites of the old tradition (most of the early presidents for example) or of descendents of slaves who took the name of their masters. Interesting in contrast to the relative scarcity of melting-pot names.[7]

In other words, whereas melting-pot names bear witness to the mongrelized and urbanized (and, for Pound, ultimately Judaized) immigrant history of the United States, the African-American proper names in the poem function as patriotic gestures toward the onomastic memory of an earlier and purer rural America. With their honorific presidential names stenciled in white (*sic*) on their green prison fatigues, the black prisoners therefore represent what is most authentic, most foundational, and, given their African rootedness in the soil, most truly "natural" and agrarian within the traditional American order: "I like a certain number of shades in my landscape" (79.31); "Their green does not swear at the landscape" (78.16); "Mr. Carver deserves mention for the / cultivation of peanuts" (74.809–10).

Paternalistic though Pound's view of blacks might have been (and today's readers will no doubt wince at his insouciantly condescending use of the terms "coon" or "nigger"), these African-American "shades" nonetheless constitute the crucial informing presence (or absence, as the case may be) behind *The Pisan Cantos*—a poem whose conflicted attitudes to race may well define its most profoundly American groundtone. As an early admirer of the blues-based poetry of Langston Hughes (with whom he corresponded about the Scottsboro Boys case), Pound noted in an unfinished radio broadcast of the early '40s, entitled "For the Afro-American Language": "One race and one race alone" has resisted "the various caucasian and semi-eastern strains" that have "thinned out the vowel sounds" and "has fostered in America a speech softer mellower and fuller than the south midland and having a charm not inferior to the 18th century phonetics preserved and tempered in our land."[8] Pound had also sought to interest Hughes in the work of the German anthropologist Leo Frobenius—who, despite the colonialist tinge of his scholarship, influenced the *négritude* poetics of Aimé Césaire and Léopold Senghor and provided the sources for the Pisans' major Africanist themes (the legend of Gassire's Lute, the messianic rebuilding of the city of Wagadu, the prosodies of African drum language, the art of the Congo and Benin masks housed in the Frobenius Institute in Frankfurt).

All of these Africanist elements converge in what is perhaps the single most moving passage of the first Canto of the Pisans, which gratefully celebrates the *humanitas* and *caritas* of a certain Mr. Edwards, the black soldier who, in violation of camp regulations, provided Pound with a table (fashioned from a packing crate) to write on in his tent. Amid the mnemonic Babel of ghostly voices besieging the poet's consciousness in his solitary confinement, this is virtually the sole recorded occasion in the entire text when he is actually addressed, in the present tense of Pisa, by another living human being. That this figure should speak as a mask (or persona) is consonant with the entire Noh theater aesthetic of the poem:

> and Mr Edwards superb green and brown
> in ward No 4 a jacent benignity,
> of the Baluba mask: "doan you tell no one
> I made you that table"
> methenamine eases the urine
> and the greatest is charity
> to be found among those who have not observed
> regulations
> (74.317–24)

Mr. Edwards' words are remembered seven Cantos later, just as the poem pre-pares to soar into its most celebrated passage ("What thou lovest well remains"):

> What counts is the cultural level,
> thank Benin for this table ex packing box
> "doan yu tell no one I made it"
> from a mask fine as any in Frankfurt
> "It'll get you offn th' groun"
> Light as the branch of Kuanon
> (81.66–71)

The ground Mr Edwards supplies is at once ethical (the exemplification of char-ity), linguistic (the black vernacular), and material (the very table Pound writes on). By a peculiarly American dialectic, however, this black ground is acknowl-edged only to be transcended (or in Hegelian terms, lifted up and canceled) by the baroque ascensional movement toward the ideal white goddess traced out a few lines later:

> Yet
> Ere the season died a-cold
> Borne upon a zephyr's shoulder
> I rose through the aureate sky
> (81.97–100).

◆ ◆ ◆

In Book X of the *Odyssey*, the "dangerous drugs" (74.414) that Circe feeds the crew make them (in W.H.D. Rouse's translation) "wholly forget their native land" and, in this condition of oblivion, they are reduced to swine. Hermes, however, provides Odysseus with the "good charm" of *moly* (whose "root was black, but the flower was milk-white') which allows him ward off the witch's *pharmaka* with memories of home. The table at which Pound the *pharmakos* (or scapegoat) rehearses his remembrances at the DTC is another such gift of trick-ster god Hermes, overstepper of boundaries, inventor of the lyre (and later, of writing), conductor of the souls of the dead into the nether world, and tradi-tionally emblematized by his enchanter's wand—the same caduceus that adorns the crate of medical or pharmaceutical supplies on which the poet now writes:

> (O Mercury god of thieves, your caduceus
> is now used by the american army
> > as witness this packing case)
> > > (77.220–23)

On this shape-shifting surface Pound began composing Cantos in late June or early July, availing himself of a pencil and a standard writing pad with wide bluish-purple rules that he had somehow acquired from the prison authorities. Featuring virtually no cross-outs or marks of erasure, this notebook—preserved at Yale's Beinecke Library along with the three others that make up the original holograph manuscript of *The Pisan Cantos*—above all reveals the rapid pace at which Pound was working during his season in hell at the DTC. Turning the pad on its side, he arrayed his text into two columns, writing as it were across the grain of the page, so that its broad rules fall vertically through the lines of his poem like so many prison bars.[9] This columnar arrangement gives rise to short, swift, heavily enjambed verse units; in the onrush of inspiration, abbreviations abound and spelling, punctuation, and quotation marks are often brushed aside:

> infantile sinthesis
> > in Barabas
> minus Hemingway -
> > minus Antheil -
> > ebullient
> by name Thomas Wilson
> Mr. K said nothing
> > foolish
> in one whole month
> > nothing foolish
> if we weren't dumb
> we wdn't be in <u>here</u> -
> > (cf. 74.99–103)

Pound's stenographic haste no doubt can in part be ascribed to the panic of "a man on whom the sun has gone down" (74.178) and who, observing the disappearance of his fellow inmates ("and Till was hung yesterday," 74.171), writes in anticipation of the possibility of his own imminent demise—hence the allusion very early on to the "Ballade des pendus" of François Villon, the mnemonic inventories of whose great serial poem, Le Testament, written in the shadow of impending death, provide a crucial model for Pound's execution of his own last will and testament at the DTC. Its deepest legacy, in lines very likely addressed to his young daughter, Mary, simply runs: "remember that I have remembered, / mia pargoletta, / and pass on the tradition" (80.452–54).

Much as he may be writing against time at the outset of the Pisans, the sheer velocity at which Pound's pencil riffs down the page nonetheless points to a compositional technique rather different from the one which had informed his previous Cantos. He had of course always been a fast worker: the previous two hundred-page installment of his epic, the Chinese and Adams Cantos, was written in only sixth months (the Adams portion in a mere five weeks).[10] But whereas Pound the historiographer was working directly from primary sources in this section of the poem, delving into the archive and constructing his text as a mosaic of transcribed citations, his detention at Pisa effectively banned him from the space of the library and forced him to draw solely on the textual capital banked in the vast storehouse of his memory. Apart from the Chinese dictionary and the edition of the Confucian Classics he had brought with him from Sant'Ambrogio, the only reading materials mentioned in The Pisan Cantos are a Bible, a missal, stray issues of Time magazine, and The Pocket Book of Verse.

On the first pages of his manuscript Pound observes "rain is also of the process / what is left is not the way" (cf. 74.13–14)—and indeed the traditional Chinese notion of tao ("way" or "process") courses through the Pisans as nowhere else in the Cantos, now revealing itself in the flux of nature, now in the humane paths of ethics, now in the metaphysical "total light process" of the neo-Confucians or Erigena.[11] But as Burton Hatlen aptly observes, however central "the process" might be to the overall imagery or philosophy of the poem, The Pisan Cantos do not simply describe this "process" but rather (in Charles Olson's term) "enact" it in the very event of their composition—a séance during which the poet takes dictation from all the various voices and personae that have been summoned to inscribe themselves on the palimpsestic writing pad (Freud's Wunderblock) of his psyche. Buoyed along by the currents and eddies of free association—Orpheus's severed head singing its way downstream?—Pound gives himself over in these notebooks to a kind of automatic writing whose meditational meanders bear comparison to the great modernist talking cures of a Beckett or Proust.

Canto 74, the first of the Pisans and, at 842 lines, by far the longest of the entire sequence, charts (somewhat like Proust's *Combray*) the struggles of a consciousness gradually trying to get its bearings in space and time as it slowly emerges from the hellhole "noman" anonymity of the Cyclops' cave (74.63), then ascends through the purgatory of the DTC and, at its close, having drunk from the waters of Lethe, is now prepared to experience the paradisal miracle of time and memory luminously regained. The holograph manuscript of this Canto, however, records a far more labyrinthine progress toward enlightenment. For example, after having defiantly affirmed "nor shall diamond die in the avalanche / be it torn from its setting / first must destroy himself ere others destroy him" (74.194–96), the voice suddenly veers into six lines of rapidly drawn Chinese characters which translate as "alone day by day alone day by day alone alone alone alone alone / alone alone alone alone alone alone alone alone alone alone, etc. ." Or, a number of pages later, this scream in Italian (to whom?): "aiuto! chiamo aiuto" ("help! I'm crying out for help!"). Most of these instances of raw vulnerability disappear in the final version of the Pisans. If they subsist at all, they are often displaced into the distancing medium of foreign languages, for whether out of Confucian decorum or some deep-seated need to elude his mother tongue, Pound's most dramatic of moments of despondency take place as it were in translation:

> J'ai eu pitié des autres
> probablement pas assez, and at moments that suited my own con-
> venience
> (76.246–47)

> lisciate con lagrime
> politis lachrymis ΔΑΚΡΥΩΝ
> (76.318–19)

> No hay amore sin celos
> Sin segreto non hay amor
> (78.203–4)

> Favonus, vento benigno
> Je suis au bout de mes forces/
> (80.659–60)

> Les larmes que j'ai créées m'inondent
> Tard, très tard je t'ai connue, la Tristesse
> I have been hard as youth sixty years
>
> > (80.674–76)

At some point, perhaps as early as mid-July, Pound was allowed special access, after taps, to the typewriter in the medical dispensary. An orderly later recalled: "The constant clanging and banging of the typewriter, which he punched angrily with his index finger, were always accompanied by a high-pitched humming sound he made as the carriage raced the bell. He swore well and profusely over typing errors."[12] Though it remains unclear whether Pound regularly typed out his day's longhand composition at night or whether he waited until he had finished several batches of Cantos before retranscribing them, Ronald Bush's examination of the Pisan typescripts has revealed that he made major cuts in Canto 74 (amounting to some 24 manuscript pages) while revising the beginning of the poem between July 14 and July 26.[13] From what one can deduce, Pound's retyping of his notebooks in these early stages not only led to a sharper delineation of the poem's overall thematic and tonal structure but, perhaps even more crucially, resulted in a more precise and expressive scoring of its words on the page—each vocable, each punctuation mark clearly zoned by two thumps (or musical rests) on the space bar:

```
Cloud  over  mountain , mountain  over  the  cloud
I  surrender  neither  the  empire  nor  the  temples
                                        plural
nor  the  constitution  nor  yet  the  city  of  Dioce
each  one  in  his  god's  name
                                        (74.336–39)
```

—the stately rallentando of which can in turn, via the typewriter, accelerate into syncopated bebop vamps:[14]

```
and  Awoi's  hennia       plays  hob  in  the  tent  flaps
          k-lakk . . . . . thuuuuuu
               making  rain
                              uuuh
2,  7,  hooo
          der  im  Baluba


     Faasa !  4 times  was  the  city  remade ,
now  in  the  heart  indestructible
                                        (77.39–46)
```

When Pound showed him the typescript of the Pisans in Washington, D.C., in early 1946, Charles Olson was above all struck by the new "methodology of verse" that Pound's kinetic "composition by field" had opened up for modernist (or, as Olson preferred to call it, "post-modernist") poetry. He later observed in his manifesto, "Projective Verse" (1950): "It is the advantage of the typewriter that, due to its rigidity and its space precisions, it can, for a poet, indicate exactly the breath, the pauses, the suspension even of syllables, the juxtapositions even of part of phrases, which he intends. For the first time the poet has the stave and the bar a musician has had."[15] And so it is in the opening movement of the Pisans, for having briefly reached the summit of Mount Purgatory by the end of Canto 74, Pound's poem leaves the domain of verbal signs altogether to move into pure musical notation: Canto 75 simply prints the score of Jannequin's Renaissance motet, "The Song of the Birds"—their paradisal jazz fully visible to the eye in the alighting of notes on the stave. Perched on the fence wires of the DTC, these songbirds return in various permutations throughout the Pisans, carefully calibrated by the typewriter:

> with 8 birds on a wire
>
> or rather on 3 wires
>
> (79.37–38)

> 5 of 'em now on 2;
>
> on 3; 7 on 4
>
> (79.74–75)

> f f
>
> d

> g
>
> write the birds in their treble scale
>
> (82.76–80)

◆ ◆ ◆

Once he had sorted out the beginning of his poem in late July, Pound proceeded at a sustained pace through the rest of summer and early fall, completing the longhand drafts of Cantos 74–83 by October 4. The first Canto had as it were prepared the palette for the rest of the sequence—or in more musical terms, had set the various subjects and countersubjects subsequently reprised in counterpoint in the larger fugue of the poem. Pound had now also discovered the broad thematic strokes that would define what in his note to the Base Censor he called the "inner shape" of his poem, a hint of which is sketched out (with tentative Canto numberings) by the following radicals on page 45 of his first notebook:

nekuia
action 74
Taishan 75
Cythera 76

Nekuia here alludes to Odysseus' descent into the underworld to consult Tiresias on the future course of his journey. Pound was convinced that this episode represented the most archaic sediment of Homer's poem, and his decision to devote Canto 1 to a translation of the *katabasis* of Book 11 of the *Odyssey* made it evident that his modernist epic would similarly have to voyage back into origins, sacrificing blood to give voice to the shades of the heroic past. Unlike the motif of descent in the earlier Cantos, however, the anamnesia enacted by the Pisans is far more internalized or subjective, turning as it does on the poet's free-associational excavation of the various buried strata of his own personal past: stray slivers of his childhood in Philadelphia and New York, fragments of his student life at Hamilton or Penn, and, most massively, elegiac shards from his early émigré years in Venice, London, and Paris, "before the world was given over to wars" (80.450). Reading through this rubble of memory in typescript, Pound's wife Dorothy worried: "Of course all these last, apparently, scraps, of cantos, are your self, the memories that make up yr. person. Is one then only a bunch of memories? i.e. a bunch of remains of contacts with the other people?"[16] And well she might have wondered, unprepared for the startlingly dispossessed "self" that emerges from the memory theater of the Pisans—less a sovereign dramaturge than the histrion of a harlequin patchwork of roles, or, as Pound presciently put it in an early poem, "a shifting change, / A broken bundle of mirrors" ("Near Perigord").

The second radical in the Pisan's design, "action"—or "the Charybdis of action" as it is pointedly called in Canto 74 in allusion to Book 12 of the *Odyssey* —situates this archetypal mythos of descent against the domain of the contingent, that is, against the perils of charting a course through the political and historical here and now. Pound famously defined his own epic as "a poem including history," and although the history included in the Pisans jump-cuts back and forth from the legendary emperors of China to the wars and revolutions of 20th-century Europe, its keenest knife-edge rests on the pulse of the present, as in the prison-diary-like calender entries marking off the Works and Days of Pound's confinement in the penal colony or in the allusions to current events gleaned from *Time* magazine or overheard on the camp's loudspeakers ("I heard it in the s.[hit] h.[ouse] a suitable place / to hear that the war was over," he writes in Canto 77 upon learning of Japan's signing of the armistice on August 14, 1945).

"Literature is news that STAYS news," Pound once quipped—and one of the most uncanny aspects of these Cantos is their author's awareness that his indictment for the capital offense of treason had now transformed him into a news item of the same collaborationist ilk as Pétain, Laval, Quisling, or Lord Haw-Haw, all of whose trials he followed in *Time* (or in *Stars and Stripes*) over the course of the summer and early fall. As Pound navigated his way through the poem, the Charybdis of his past actions as a broadcaster for Mussolini's Italy therefore constantly threatened to wreck the momentum of his text toward some sort of resolution or closure. But whether by wily prevarication or obdurate blindness, its pages remain silent about the moral or political implications of their author's past pro-Fascist or anti-Semitic discourses—remorse for these utterances would not fully strike Pound until the Learlike muteness of his final years. In these Cantos, by contrast, the contrition expressed is almost entirely reserved for the jealous entanglements of his domestic life. As for the Charybis of his present legal plight—was his ongoing imprisonment in the DTC due to a "double X or burocracy" (74.456)?—he would attempt to "salmon thru" its straits as best he could (79.26), even if this eventually involved acquiescence to a slippery plea of insanity to escape trial.

"Taishan," the third radical in the poem's design, refers to the highest peak in the Apennine range overlooking the plain of Pisa from the east, so named by Pound in honor of the "Great Mountain" in Confucius's native Shantung province, traditionally sacred to the Chinese because believed to control man's fate on earth. As opposed to the historical and political contingencies of the realm of "action," Taishan in these Cantos represents the immanent domain of Nature, providing a distant point of reference that gathers the entire landscape below into its Oriental grandeur:

> and there was a smell of mint under the tent flaps
> especially after the rain
>   and a white ox on the road toward Pisa
>   as if facing the tower,
> dark sheep in the drill field and on wet days were clouds
> in the mountain as if under the guard roosts.

> A lizard upheld me
> the wild birds wd not eat the white bread
> from Mt Taishan to the sunset
>
> (74.120–28)

Ever sensitive to the changing play of light and clouds around Taishan (as if to read therein the signs of his own fate?), the poet records the mutability of his own moods as they shift from dusk to dawn:

> one day were clouds banked on Taishan
> or in glory of sunset
> and tovarish blessed without aim
> wept in the rainditch at evening
> (74.182–85)

> and Mt Taishan is faint as the wraith of my first friend
> who comes talking ceramics;
> mist glaze over mountain
> (77.51–53)

> there is no base seen under Taishan
> but the brightness of 'udor   ὕδωρ
> the poplar tips float in brightness
> only the stockade posts stand

> And now the ants seem to stagger
> as the dawn sun has trapped their shadows,
> this breath wholly covers the mountains
> it shines and divides
> it nourishes by its rectitude
> does no injury
> (83. 83–92)

The joyous dawn songs of the Pisans reach all the way back to Pound's earliest translations of Provençal *albas*, but what distinguishes the imagistic landscape poetry of these Cantos from all his previous verse is the way in which the immediacies of nature, minutely observed—the smell of mint after the rain, the Tuscan birds refusing Yankee white bread, the stagger of ants' shadows—are profiled against a world irrevocably lost or reduced to ruin ("beyond the stockade there is chaos and nothingness," 80.284). Yet it is precisely the limited field of the poet's vision—confined to the peep-hole of his tent, circumscribed by the stockade, his horizon bounded to the east by Taishan and to the south by the Tower of Pisa—that allows him to map his immediate surroundings as a pastoral *locus amoenus*, each of whose tiniest inhabitants, be they a katydid (74.356), spider (76.276), or cricket (78.107), deserves grateful attention:

> When the mind swings by a grass-blade
> an ant's forefoot shall save you
> (83.144–45)

It is at moments like these that, despite their fractured postmodernist surface, *The Pisan Cantos* rejoin the most traditional impulses of elegy: grief transmuted into consolation, the work of mourning at last finding solace in the regenerative energies of Nature.

"Cythera"—thus named for the island where Aphrodite first stepped ashore from her foam-borne shell—provides the final element in the Pisan's initial design. As the goddess of beauty, she appears early in the sequence in her traditional aesthetic guises, now painted by Botticelli, now by the Pre-Raphaelites, now glimpsed in a snapshot memory of Olga Rudge:

> she did her hair in small ringlets, à la 1880 it might have been,
> red, and the dress she wore Drecol or Lanvin
> a great goddess, Aeneas knew her forthwith
> (74.363–65)

Most frequently, however, she visits the poet as a fluid, diaphanous body whose crystalline ethereality offers a Dantescan promise of redemption through the power of love—a realization only fully achieved at the outset of Canto 80: "Amo ergo sum, and in just that proportion." Indeed, as the poem moves from late summer into early fall, the goddess gradually expands to encompass all of Nature, her love now permeating the three elements of air (Canto 80), earth (Canto 82), and water (Canto 83). As Venus the morning star, she appears as the consort of Mt. Taishan:

> Taishan is attended of loves
> under Cythera, before sunrise
> (81.2–3)

And under her influence, the entire Pisan landscape is eroticized into a soft-focus projection of her giant body:

> Mist covers the breasts of Tellus-Helena and drifts up the Arno
>
> (77.281)

Syncretically fused with the archaic earth-mothers Gea and Tellus and with the figures of Demeter and Persephone, Pound's Cythera participates (through her inconsolable grief for the vegetation deity, Adonis) in the great Eleusinian fertility rites of Canto 79 and finally, at the end of Canto 82, invites the poet into her chthonic embrace—with the *nekuia* motif of descent and return, of seasonal death and rebirth here reaching its most fully erotic expression:

> How drawn, O GEA TERRA
> > what draws as thou drawest
> > > till one sink into thee by an arm's width
> > embracing thee. Drawest,
> > > truly thou drawest.
> > Wisdom lies next thee,
> > > simply, past metaphor.
> Where I lie let the thyme rise
> > > and basilicum
> > let the herbs rise in April abundant
> >
> > (82.99–108)

Behind these lines stands the shade of Walt Whitman, whose *Leaves of Grass* enter the poem at this juncture from the pages of M.E. Speare's *Pocket Book of Verse*, recently discovered by chance "on the jo-house seat" (80.663). Awash though his memory had been with scraps of Greek, Latin, Provençal, Italian, French, Spanish, and Portuguese verse in the earlier Pisans, Pound's encounter with this paperback anthology of "Great English and American Poems"—from which his own work is noticeably absent—provides something of an intertextual jolt to Canto 80, inspiring a parody of Browning's "Home Thoughts from Abroad" and an homage to the stanzaic form of Fitzgerald's *Rubáiyát of Omar Khayyám* in preparation for the great prosodic climax of the following Canto ("What thou lov'st well remains"). Hugh Kenner's meticulous analysis of the "drama of meter" enacted by Canto 81 stands unsurpassed: "A process has traversed in half a page the history of English versification from Chaucer to 1945, decasyllabic becoming pentameter, pentameter encountering

Imagist resistance, and metaphorphosing into the idiosyncratically stressed line that carries Pound's hallmark."[17]

"To write dialog because there is / no one to converse with" (80.236–37). In addition to the spirited conversation with the English verse tradition inaugurated by his discovery of Professor Speare's anthology in September, the Pisan notebooks disclose that Pound was also moving into closer colloquy with the Confucian Classic, Ta Hio, whose translation he undertook during this same month and in the same writing pad—so that if one turns over page 252 of the manuscript ("Pull down thy vanity") one finds page 18 of The Great Digest running in reverse in English. This double process of digestion—which involves both the nutritive assimilation of the history of the English line by mimetic rewriting and, via the kindred act of translation, the gathering of philosophical sustenance from the "totalitarian" political and social axioms of the Ta Hio— may explain Pound's remark in a later letter that his "lesion of May" had been "cured" at Pisa "in Sept"(even though he feared it might again "bust open under the renewed fatigues").[18] But whatever the ultimate causes of this "cure," a new resolve seems to animate the poem as it advances into September. In Canto 78, for example, Aeneas (son of Venus) replaces the wandering Odysseus as the poem's central figure of exile; the allusions to the former's journey from Troy to Latium indicate a desire to move beyond the elegiac poetics of personal loss into the messianic anticipation of the ideal city (or temple), "now in the mind indestructible," that will rearise out of the catastrophe of history—either as the reincarnation of foundational Rome or as the resurrection of Pound's (wholly delusional) dream of Mussolini's short-lived Republic of Salò.

This mounting level of prophetic confidence (further heightened by the hymnic lynx choruses of Canto 79, written in celebration of his wife Dorothy's birthday on September 14) informs the most celebrated—and most controversial—passage in the poem, namely the "Pull down thy vanity" section of Canto 81. Long taken by critics to represent Pound's crowning moment of confessional insight into his own tragic hubris, more recent readings have suggested precisely the opposite, arguing that this jeremiad is in no sense self-reflexive but entirely directed to the "other"—the vanity in this case being imputable not to the poet himself but rather to the corrupt social order that has, in violation of Nature, produced the latest war and, more particularly, fostered the American army's vainglorious imperial ambitions.[19] Although the latter interpretation seems to have gained ground, both readings remain simultaneously plausible, for it is a particular feature of Pound's schizopoetics (as Deleuzians might call them) that the positions of self and other, subject and object, remain ever unstable, ever convertible. Even at its most metrically and rhetorically assertive (as in this passage), Pound's verse is richest when moving within its own space of self-contradiction.[20]

What does remain clear from Canto 81, however, is the extent to which Pound is trying to guide his nomadic poem of exile toward some sort of sort of homecoming. The "suave eyes" of the first line of Canto 74 now return, glimpsed as if amid a troupe of carnival maskers:

> there came a new subtlety of eyes into my tent,
> whether of spirit or hypostasis,
> but what the blindfold hides
> or at carneval
> nor any pair showed anger
> Saw but the eyes and stance between the eyes
> (81.118–23)

And the question posed a few lines thereafter—"Whose world, or mine or theirs / or is it of none?"—is finally answered in the affirmative two Cantos later, with the same eyes revisiting the poet and at last triumphantly inscribing the power of their gaze onto his heart. In this ecstatic moment of ocular reversal (borrowed from Cavalcanti), outer and inner visions cross over into each other to reemerge as the fulfilled mirror image of Love:

> The eyes, this time my world
> But pass and look *from* mine
> between my lids
> sea, sky, and pool
> alternate
> pool, sky, sea
> (83.197–202)

And on this quietly meditative note Pound moved his poem to a close.

◆ ◆ ◆

In mid-September, after having been held incommunicado for nearly four months, Pound was finally given permission to correspond with his wife; he sent her a typed version of Canto 81 ("more human than a dull letter") and announced the completion of the entire sequence on October 2: "I have done a Decad 74/83 (about 80 pages in this typescript)." Further fragments of the poem were sent to Dorothy to be relayed on to Olga and daughter Mary at Sant'

Ambrogio for retyping—even Pound's agèd mother, Isabel, was given bits to read (her withering reaction, according to Dorothy: "after five months undisturbed (sic) I expected something more valuable").[21] But even as he continued to get the typescript of the Pisans into shape, his energies were now directed else-where—namely to the translation of the Confucian Classics *The Great Digest* and *The Unwobbling Pivot*, both of which he considered essential to the legacy he needed leave to posterity from the death cells of Pisa.[22] On October 8, how-ever, Pound received word from Dorothy that J.P. Angold, a young poet-econo-mist he very much admired, had been killed while on active service in the RAF, and the shock of this belated piece of news, stirring up memories of the battle-field death of his close friend Henri Gaudier-Brzeska in 1915, reopened a deep gash of unconsummated mourning which he proceeded to work out in one last Canto, interweaving Bertran de Born's lament for the young king Henry into a dirge for the fallen pilot.

Ronald Bush's careful examination of the manuscripts and typescripts of this final Canto shows just how difficult it was for Pound to suture the angry wound opened up by Angold's death; indeed, he continued to revise this coda as late as November 14, hesitating between rage and resignation.[23] Current events, at any rate, were quickly catching up with the poet: in an October 1 issue of *Time* mag-azine (mentioned in this Canto) he learned that the radio broadcaster William Joyce (also known as "Lord Haw Haw" and with whom he had briefly corre-sponded in the '40s) had been found guilty of treason and sentenced to be hanged. And later that month he learned from Dorothy that both Pierre Laval and Vidkun Quisling had been executed for treason; their deaths, along with those of other Fascist "martyrs," are saluted halfway through the Canto in a cryp-tic threnody ("Xaire"=Hail or Heil):

> Xaire Alessandro
>   Xaire Fernando, e il Capo,
> Pierre, Vidkun,
>   Henriot
>
> (84.77–80)

Early in November Pound also learned from *Stars and Stripes* that six Italian radio technicians were about to be flown to Washington to testify at a grand-jury investigation of his case. According to eyewitness Robert Allen: "His last two weeks at the DTC were the most difficult for him. His tone of conversation changed and occasionally he spoke of himself in the past tense. Several times he said, 'If I go down, someone must carry on.'"[24]

It is against this background of grief, fear, and mounting defiance that Pound's final revision of the poem at the DTC must be situated—a revision that completely reframed the eleven Cantos, explicitly transforming the entire sequence into a requiem for Italian Fascism. As Ronald Bush has discovered, Pound withheld the deep object of his mourning in the Pisans until the bitter end, for in the second week of November (perhaps no longer worried about the Base Censor) he radically changed the opening of the poem, inserting the following lines, held in abeyance on a stray piece of toilet paper (see frontispiece), as its new incipit:

> The enormous tragedy of the dream in the peasant's bent
> shoulders
> Manes! Manes was tanned and stuffed,
> Thus Ben and la Clara *a Milano*
>   by the heels at Milano
> That maggots shd/ eat the dead bullock
> Digonos, **Δίγονος**, but the twice crucified
>   where in history will you find it?

Instead of embarking under the compassionate gaze of the goddess ("The suave eyes, quiet, not scornful"), the eleven Cantos now bear the inaugural weight of the defiled and inverted corpse of Mussolini—whose unofficial title, Il Duce, often translated by Pound as "the Boss," evokes the sacrificial slaying of twice-born Dionysos in the form of a bull (*bos* in Latin), here devoured by the maggotlike *partigiani* responsible for his murder. Allegorically displacing history into myth and supplanting the divine visitations of Love with the violent logic of sacrifice, Pound at a single stroke transforms a poem of elegy (or even comedy, in Dante's deepest sense) into one that must bear witness to "the enormous tragedy" of Italy's Fascist dream—a burden of tragic vision hardly supported by the body of the text, whose open and Odyssean form now undergoes a final and truculent political closure.[25]

On November 16, shortly after revising and retyping the beginning of his poem, Pound received word he was going to be flown back to Washington to stand trial. Eyewitness Robert Allen again: "One evening after taps in the middle of November, Pound was sitting in the dispensary reading Joseph E. Davies' *Mission to Moscow*. The Charge of Quarters sat at the desk next to him. From time to time Pound commented on the book. Suddenly the door opened and two young lieutenants entered. They told Pound that he would be flown to Washington in one hour and to get his personal effects together. They turned and left. Pound handed the book to the C. Q. He asked them to thank all of the medical personnel for their kindness. He then walked to the door of the prefab, turned, with a half-smile, put both hands around his neck to form a noose and jerked up his chin." Upon his arrival in Washington, Pound was placed in the District of Columbia Jail. At his preliminary arraignment on November 19, he asked to act as his own counsel, but was informed by Judge Bolitha Laws that the charge of treason against him was too serious for him to undertake his own defense. At the suggestion of his publisher, James Laughlin, Pound agreed to retain the services of Julien Cornell, a Quaker civil liberties lawyer with experience in representing conscientious objectors and pacifists. At his formal arraignment on November 27 (for nineteen overt acts of treasonous broadcasting), Cornell advised Pound to stand mute and entered a plea of not guilty on his behalf, arguing that his client was "not sufficiently well to enter a plea." On December 4, Pound was transferred to Gallinger Hospital for examination and observation by four psychiatrists. The patient complained that he was experiencing "a queer sensation in the head as though the upper third of the brain were missing and a fluid level existed at the top of what remained," and in a December 12 report, drafted by Dr. Winfred Overholser, the medical panel concluded that Pound, suffering from "a paranoid state," was "insane and mentally unfit for trial" and "in need of care in a mental hospital."[26]

At Judge Laws' recommendation, Pound was transferred to St. Elizabeths Federal Hospital for the Insane on December 21, where he was placed in solitary confinement in Howard Hall, a penal ward, pending the jury hearing on his sanity—which, after many postponements, finally took place on February 13. Although cheered by the visits of Charles Olson ("Olson saved my life"), these seven weeks in the "hell hole" of Howard Hall, according to Pound, reopened the "lesion" he had experienced in his prison cage at Pisa in May and had "busted" his "main spring." In a letter to his daughter, Mary, he recalled Circe's instructions to Odysseus from the *nekuia* of Canto 47: "First must thou go the road / to hell / And to the bower of Ceres' daughter Proserpine, / Through overhanging dark, to see Tiresias, / Eyeless that was, a shade, that is in hell." And to his lawyer Julien Cornell, giving his address as "Dungeon," he scrawled the following in late January:

> mental torture
> constitution a religion
> a world lost
> grey mist barrier impas[s]ible
> ignorance absolute
> anonyme

> futility of might have been
> coherent areas
>   constantly
>   invaded
>   aiuto
>   Pound

But even though he informed his doctors that "I am so shot to pieces that it would take me years to write a sensible piece of prose," he was still somehow able to focus on his poem, for it was during this period of incarceration in the "snake pit," fighting off fits of claustrophobia, that he made the final revisions to the typescript he had brought back from Pisa in preparation for its submission to New Directions and Faber & Faber.

At Pound's sanity hearing on February 13, after listening to the expert psychiatric testimony, the jury returned a verdict that the respondent was of "unsound mind"—a somewhat Pyrrhic victory for Cornell, for while it protected Pound from prosecution for the nonce, the indictment for treason remained in effect until such a time as the accused had recovered sufficient sanity to stand trial. In this juridical limbo—neither innocent or guilty and because adjudged *non compos mentis*, no longer a legal subject with power of signature—Pound would reside at St Elizabeths for the next twelve years. In the temporary euphoria of the moment, however, "with his bounce back," Pound jubilantly showed Charles Olson the freshly retyped manuscript of Cantos 74–84 he received from New Directions on Valentine's Day.[27] Reperusing the clean typescript of the poem, he wrote to Dorothy, "I long for Pisan paradise," and to another correspondent, "I miss the Pisan paradise like hell." Laughlin, however, was in no hurry to publish the text: its author was being pilloried in the press (his case often compared to that of the recently executed Lord Haw-Haw) and with the general cries for blood, the publisher adopted a wait-and-see attitude, mollifying Pound by printing his Confucian translations, *The Great Digest* and *The Unwobbling Pivot*, in March of the following year—a relatively uncontroversial move, even though Pound insisted that they constituted a crucial exhibit for his defense.

On July 30, 1948, New Directions finally issued Cantos 74–84 under the title *The Pisan Cantos*—the Faber and Faber edition would be delayed for another full year while its editors, fearful of Britain's stringent libel laws, made a number of expurgations in the text. In November a committee of poets met in Washington to deliberate about the awarding of a newly created literary prize funded by philanthropist Paul Mellon of the Bollingen Foundation (so named after the Swiss home of C.G. Jung) and administered, at Allen Tate's suggestion, by the Poetry Consultant of the Library of Congress in collaboration with the Library's board of Fellows in American Literature. Léonie Adams, that year's Poetry Consultant at the Library, chaired the proceedings, while the judges included current fellows Conrad Aiken, W. H. Auden, Louise Bogan, Katherine Garrison Chapin (whose husband, former Attorney General Francis Biddle, had indicted Pound for treason in 1943), T.S. Eliot, Robert Lowell, Karl Shapiro, and Allen Tate. At their meeting, and to no one's great surprise, given Tate's behind-the-scenes maneuverings and the intimidating presence of recent Nobel Laureate T.S. Eliot, *The Pisan Cantos* emerged as the major contender for the $10,000 Bollingen Prize, with William Carlos Williams' *Paterson* (*Book 2*) its nearest competitor. In the initial ballot, eight votes were recorded for Pound's book, three for Williams' (Shapiro, Aiken, and Chapin), with two abstentions. A second postal vote was taken the following February, with Shapiro pointedly abstaining. In its press release of February 20, the Library of Congress included the following statement by the jury: "The fellows are aware that objections may be made to awarding a prize to a man situated as is Mr. Pound. . . . To permit other considerations than that of poetic achievement to sway the decision would destroy the significance of the award and would in principle deny the validity of that objective perception of value on which civilized society must rest."

A firestorm followed. *The New York Times* headline: "POUND, IN MENTAL CLINIC, / WINS PRIZE FOR POETRY / PENNED IN TREASON CELL." Radio Moscow: "One is prompted to ask how low and miserable must be the quality of modern bourgeois poetry in America if even the insane and verified ravings of a confessed madman could win a literary prize?" Robert Hillyer in the *Saturday Review* linked Pound's Fascism to the Nazi leanings of Jung's circle and insinuated that aluminum tycoon Paul Mellon, in cahoots with the fellows of the Library of Congress, was engaging in "the mystical and cultural preparation for the new authoritarianism." Other magazines soon joined into the fray. Those sympathetic to New Criticism (*Poetry, Sewanee Review, Hudson Review, New Republic, Harper's*) supported the jury's insistence on "poetic achievement" as the sole criterion for the award. A far broader majority (ranging from *Masses* and *Mainstream* to *Catholic World, Partisan Review, Atlantic,* and *Time*) denounced Pound as a traitor and anti-Semite, criticizing what George Orwell termed the fellows' "art for art's sake position. . . that aesthetic integrity and common decency are two separate things."[28] But as Jed Rasula has observed in his excellent analysis of the entire controversy, even as these various arguments assumed the form of the traditional debate between form and content (raising the question whether Plato was indeed right in calling for the expulsion of poets from the Republic), the real issue in fact revolved around the institutional and fiduciary power of the Eliotic New Critics to underwrite the symbolic credit of high modernist poetry on the American cultural and university scene: "What was crucial was the preservation of the administrative security system that had assumed custodial control of poetry (not just Pound's poetry) as surely as the man was impounded in a mental asylum."[29] As for "the man that lay in the house of Bedlam" (in Elizabeth Bishop's phrase), he prepared a short press statement which he then decided not to issue: "No comment from the bughouse."

◆ ◆ ◆

Thanks to the concerted efforts of Archibald MacLeish, Robert Frost, Ernest Hemingway, and T.S. Eliot, the Justice Department finally agreed to release Pound from St. Elizabeths on May 7, 1958—without trial. That summer, accompanied by his wife Dorothy and his young secretary Marcella Spann, he moved to his daughter's castle in the South Tyrol. Eight months later, suffering from the altitude and depressed by internecine tensions at Brunnenburg ("Pride, jealousy and possessiveness / 3 pains of hell," Canto 113), he returned to Rapallo. In May, he set off with Dorothy and Marcella on a short tour of Italy, his first such excursion in fifteen years. The first stop he insisted on making was the village of Metato, just north of Pisa, his "paradiso perduto."[30] The cages were gone, and in their place lay a rose nursery.

1   The biographical information about Pound's arrest and subsequent captivity at Pisa has been primarily derived from the following sources: Humphrey Carpenter, *A Serious Character: The Life of Ezra Pound* (Boston: Houghton Mifflin, 1988), *Ezra and Dorothy Pound: Letters in Captivity 1945–1946*, ed. Omar Pound and Robert Spoo (New York: Oxford University Press, 1999), *A Casebook on Ezra Pound*, ed. William Van O'Connor and Edward Stone (New York: Thomas Y. Crowell, 1959).

2   See Wendy Stallard Flory, "Confucius against Confusion: Ezra Pound and the Catholic Chaplain at Pisa," in *Ezra Pound and China*, ed. Zhaoming Qian (Ann Arbor: University of Michigan Press, 2003), pp. 143–62.

3   See Robert Casillo, "Fascists of the Final Hour: Pound's Italian Cantos," in *Fascism, Aesthetics, and Culture*, ed. Richard J. Golsan (Hanover: University Press of New England, 1992), pp. 98–127.

4   See Ronald Bush, "'Quiet, Not Scornful?': The Composition of the *Pisan Cantos*," in *A Poem Including History: The Cantos of Ezra Pound*, ed. Lawrence Rainey (Ann Arbor: University of Michigan Press, 1996), pp. 169–211, as well as his "Towards Pisa: More from the Archives about Pound's Italian Cantos," *Agenda* (Spring 1998), pp. 89–124. Translations of the typescripts of the Italian Cantos 74 and 75 are also included in Massimo Bacigalupo, "Ezra Pound's Cantos 72 and 73: An Annotated Translation," *Paideuma* XX, 1 & 2 (Spring–Fall 1991), pp. 11–41.

5   Charles Olson and Robert Creeley, *The Complete Correspondence*, ed. George F. Butterick (Santa Barbara: Black Sparrow Press, 1980), vol. I, p. 92. Quoted by Burton Hatlen, "Pound's *Pisan Cantos* and the Origins of Projective Verse," in *Ezra Pound and Poetic Influence*, ed. Helen Dennis (Amsterdam: Rodolpi, 2000), p. 13.

6   See Toni Morrison's discussion of "black surrogacy" in *Playing in the Dark: Whiteness and the Literary Imagination* (New York: Vintage Books, 1993), pp. 7–19.

7   Dated November 4. Reproduced in *Ezra Pound and Dorothy Pound: Letters in Captivity*, p. 177.

8   This unfinished piece is quoted and discussed both by Jonathan Gill and Alec Marsh in "Ezra Pound and African American Modernism," a special issue of *Paideuma*, XXIX, 1 & 2 (Spring–Fall 2000), pp. 84 and 130. See also Michael North, *The Dialect of Modernism: Race, Language and Twentieth-Century Literature* (New York: Oxford University Press, 1994).

9   The first notebook contains the initial portion of Canto 74 and is numbered pp. 1–78. The second notebook continues this same Canto (MS pp.79–111) and consists of a regular ruled stationery pad whose front cover reads "Harlich's Writing Vellum" and whose back cover provides the calendars for 1943 and 1944 with the U.S. Army insignia. The text is written sideways in two columns until p. 85 and then without columns thereafter. The third notebook containing Cantos 74–80 (MS pp. 112–81) is neatly written in regular horizontal fashion (and in longer lines) on an unruled airmail stationery pad whose cover reads "Stratosphere / Air Weight Paper / Postage Save." The fourth notebook, which includes Cantos 80–83 (MS pp. 182–283), is identical to the first notebook and is also written perpendicularly across the blue rules in two columns. The text of the Pisans occupies the recto, but flipping the notebook over, Pound started at the back and wrote out his translation of the *Ta Hio* on the unruled verso until he reached p. 18, at which point he resumed his composition of Cantos on the verso. A final "Notebook E," identical to the previous one, entitled "The Great Digest" and dated "Sept. 8 1945 Pisa," contains further notes for Pound's translation of the Confucian text.

10 See Ronald Bush, "'Quiet, Not Scornful?'", p. 171, and Burton Hatlen, "Pound's *Pisan Cantos* and the Origins of Projective Verse," pp. 146–50. Both of these essays have been crucial to my understanding of the composition of the Pisans, and I have relied on them extensively in my account.

11 See Hugh Kenner, *The Pound Era* (Berkeley: University of California Press, 1971), pp. 445–59, for an etymological account of the Confucian Pound's unwitting Taoism. Anthony Woodward, *Ezra Pound and the Pisan Cantos* (London: Routledge & Kegan Paul, 1980), pp. 22–37, provides a useful discussion of the role of process in the poem, linking its *tao* both to its neo-Platonic mysticism and its "light from Eleusis," especially evident in the fertility rituals evoked in Cantos 79 and 83.

12 Robert L. Allen, "The Cage," in A Casebook on Ezra Pound, p. 36

13 See his booklength study of The Composition of "The Pisan Cantos," forthcoming from Oxford University Press.

14 As Pound is composing the Pisans in the summer of 1945, Charlie Parker, Dizzy Gillespie, and Max Roach are inventing bebop on 52nd Street. Parker records his historic performance of "Ko Ko" for Savoy Records on November 26, 1945, the same day Pound is officially reindicted for treason in Washington, D.C. Like Bird, Pound plays manic changes in the Pisans—taking apart verbal chords and redistributing their elements, according to Olson, "like a wild speed-machine."

15 Charles Olson, Selected Writings, ed. Robert Creeley (New York: New Directions, 1966), p. 22. Quoted and admirably discussed in Hatlen, "Pound's Pisan Cantos and the Origins of Projective Verse." The original 1948 New Directions printing of The Pisan Cantos—the title was the publisher's, not Pound's—attempted to reproduce as faithfully as possible the idiosyncrasies of the typescript. All the double-spacing between words, however, was eliminated and its erratic left margins and indents were often regularized. In addition, the original typescript contained far many more Chinese characters than the final printed version: James Laughlin's balking at the expense of reproducing this welter of ideograms was among the several factors that delayed the publication of the book until July 1948. See Ronald Bush, "Confucius Erased: The Missing Ideograms in The Pisan Cantos," in Ezra Pound and China, pp. 163–92.

16 Ezra and Dorothy Pound: Letters in Captivity, p.131.

17 The Pound Era, pp. 486–93.

18 Letter to Ronald Duncan of November 25, 1945, quoted in Ezra and Dorothy Pound: Letters in Captivity, p. 23. For an excellent discussion of Pound's "totalitarian Confucianism," see Mary Paterson Cheadle, Ezra Pound's Confucian Translations (Ann Arbor: University of Michigan Press, 1997), pp. 57–114.

19 See Peter d'Epiro, "Whose Vanity Must Be Pulled Down," Paideuma, XIII, 2 (Fall 1984), pp. 252ff.

20 See Jean-Michel Rabaté, Language, Sexuality and Ideology in Ezra Pound's Cantos (Albany: State University of New York Press, 1986), pp. 141–82, and Jerome McGann, Towards a Literature of Knowledge (Chicago: University of Chicago Press, 1989), p. 112ff.

21 Ezra and Dorothy Pound: Letters in Captivity, pp. 101 and 133. Compare the acumen of Olga Rudge's comment in her October 9th letter: "I felt it the best thing they could have done for the Cantos, to shut you up for a while. She is glad he has begun to sing again." Quoted in Anne Conover, Olga Rudge & Ezra Pound (New Haven: Yale University Press, 2001), p. 166.

22 The Great Digest (dated "D.T.C. Pisa; 5 October–5 November, 1945") and The Unwobbling Pivot were published as a single issue of New Directions' Pharos magazine in 1947, some fourteen months before The Pisan Cantos saw print.

23 Bush, " 'Quiet, Not Scornful?'", pp. 198–201.

24 Robert L. Allen, "The Cage," pp. 37–38. The euphoria inspired by Dorothy's visit to the camp on October 2 (with Olga and daughter Mary following two weeks later) was offset by a growing impatience with the military authorities. On November 3, Pound wrote the DTC's new commander, Major Morris J. Lucree: "In view of the situation in China and Japan, it seems to me that the bottling of my knowledge now amounts to suppression of military information." Ezra and Dorothy Pound: Letters in Captivity, p. 171.

25 The movement from elegy or epic into (revenge) tragedy will only be truly enacted in Pound's subsequent translations at St. Elizabeths of Sophocles' Elektra and Women of Trachis, in which the memory of Mussolini inhabits the slain bodies of Agammenon and Hercules. For Pound's ongoing allegiance to the castrated phallus of Mussolini, see Wolfgang Schivelbusch, The Culture of Defeat: On National Trauma, Mourning, and Recovery (New York: Henry Holt, 2003).

26 The details of Pound's nostos to Washington are taken from Carpenter, A Serious Character, and Pound and Spoo, Ezra and Dorothy Pound: Letters in Captivity.

27 Charles Olson & Ezra Pound: An Encounter at St. Elizabeths, ed. Catherine Seelye (New York: Grossman Publishers, 1975), p.72

28 Orwell's comments come from the forum on the "Pound Award" published in *Partisan Review* in May 1949. Other participants included W.H. Auden, Robert Gorham Davis, Clement Greenberg, Irving Howe, George Orwell, Karl Shapiro, Allen Tate, and William Barrett. Reprinted in *A Casebook on Ezra Pound*, pp. 54–66, and incisively discussed by Marjorie Perloff, "Fascism, Anti-Semitism, Isolationism: Contextualizing the 'Case of E.P.'" *Paideuma* XVI, 3 (Winter 1987), pp. 7–21.

29 Jed Rasula, *The American Poetry Wax Museum: Reality Effects, 1940–1990* (Urbana: NCCTE, 1996), p. 114.

30 Doodling on a subscription form in 1946, Pound gave his nationality as "paradiso perduto." *Ezra and Dorothy Pound: Letters in Captivity*, p. 32.

▪ THE PISAN CANTOS ▪

LXXIV–LXXXIV

LXXIV

THE enormous tragedy of the dream in the peasant's bent
        shoulders
        Manes! Manes was tanned and stuffed,
        Thus Ben and la Clara *a Milano*
5   by the heels at Milano
That maggots shd/ eat the dead bullock
DIGONOS, Δίγονος, but the twice crucified
                where in history will you find it?
yet say this to the Possum: a bang, not a whimper,
10   with a bang not with a whimper,
To build the city of Dioce whose terraces are the colour of stars.
The suave eyes, quiet, not scornful,
                    rain also is of the process.
What you depart from is not the way
15   and olive tree blown white in the wind
washed in the Kiang and Han
what whiteness will you add to this whiteness,
                            what candor?
" the great periplum brings in the stars to our shore."
20   You who have passed the pillars and outward from Herakles
when Lucifer fell in N. Carolina.
if the suave air give way to scirocco
ΟΫ ΤΙΣ, ΟΫ ΤΙΣ? Odysseus
                the name of my family.
25   the wind also is of the process,
                        sorella la luna
Fear god and the stupidity of the populace,
but a precise definition
        transmitted thus Sigismundo
30   thus Duccio, thus Zuan Bellin, or trastevere with La Sposa
Sponsa Cristi in mosaic till our time / deification of emperors

but a snotty barbarian ignorant of T'ang history need not deceive
one

nor Charlie Sung's money on loan from anonimo
35   that is, we suppose Charlie had some

and in India the rate down to 18 per hundred
but the local loan lice provided from imported bankers
so the total interest sweated out of the Indian farmers
       rose in Churchillian grandeur
40   as when, and plus when, he returned to the putrid gold standard
as was about 1925   Oh my England
that free speech without free radio speech is as zero
       and but one point needed for Stalin
you need not, i.e. need not take over the means of production;
45   money to signify work done, inside a system
       and measured and wanted
" I have not done unnecessary manual labour "
says the R. C. chaplain's field book
            (preparation before confession)
50   squawky as larks over the death cells
            militarism progressing westward
im Westen nichts neues
and the Constitution in jeopardy
and that state of things not very new either

55   " of sapphire, for this stone giveth sleep "
not words whereto to be faithful
       nor deeds that they be resolute
          only that bird-hearted equity make timber
          and lay hold of the earth
60   and Rouse found they spoke of Elias
in telling the tales of Odysseus   ΟΥ ΤΙΣ
            ΟΥ ΤΙΣ
" I am noman, my name is noman "
but Wanjina is, shall we say, Ouan Jin
65   or the man with an education

4 ∎

and whose mouth was removed by his father
               because he made too many *things*
whereby cluttered the bushman's baggage
vide the expedition of Frobenius' pupils about 1938
70   to Auss 'ralia
Ouan Jin spoke and thereby created the named
                            thereby making **clutter**
the bane of men moving
and so his mouth was removed
75 as you will find it removed in his pictures
                         in principio verbum
            paraclete or the verbum perfectum: **sinceritas**
from the death cells in sight of Mt. Taishan @ Pisa
as Fujiyama at Gardone
80 when the cat walked the top bar of the railing
and the water was still on the West side
flowing toward the Villa Catullo
where with sound ever moving
                    in diminutive poluphloisboios
85 in the stillness outlasting all wars
" La Donna " said Nicoletti
                   " la donna,
                         la donna! "
" Cosa deve continuare? "
90 " Se casco " said Bianca Capello
" non casco in ginnocchion "
and with one day's reading a man may have the key in his hands
Lute of Gassir. Hooo Fasa
came a lion-coloured pup bringing fleas
95 and a bird with white markings, a stepper
                      under *les six potences*
Absouldre, que tous nous vueil absoudre
lay there Barabbas and two thieves lay beside him
infantile synthesis in Barabbas
100 minus Hemingway, minus Antheil, ebullient

and by name Thos. Wilson
Mr K. said nothing foolish, the whole month nothing foolish:
" if we weren't dumb, we wouldn't be here "
                              and the Lane gang.
105   Butterflies, mint and Lesbia's sparrows,
the voiceless with bumm drum and banners,
                              and the ideogram of the guard roosts
el triste pensier si volge
          ad Ussel. A Ventadour
110   va il consire, el tempo rivolge
and at Limoges the young salesman
bowed with such french politeness " No that is impossible."
I have forgotten which city
But the caverns are less enchanting to the unskilled explorer
115   than the Urochs as shown on the postals,
we will see those old roads again, question,
                              possibly
but nothing appears much less likely,
                              Mme Pujol,
120   and there was a smell of mint under the tent flaps
especially after the rain
                    and a white ox on the road toward Pisa
                    as if facing the tower,
dark sheep in the drill field and on wet days were clouds
125   in the mountain as if under the guard roosts.
                    A lizard upheld me
                    the wild birds wd not eat the white bread
                    from Mt Taishan to the sunset
From Carrara stone to the tower
130   and this day the air was made open
          for Kuanon of all delights,
                Linus, Cletus, Clement
                              whose prayers,
the great scarab is bowed at the altar
135   the green light gleams in his shell

plowed in the sacred field and unwound the silk worms early
　　　　　　　　　　　　　　　　in tensile
in the light of light is the *virtù*
　　　　　　" sunt lumina " said Erigena Scotus 顯
140　　　　　　as of Shun on Mt Taishan
and in the hall of the forebears
　　　　　　　　　　as from the beginning of wonders
the paraclete that was present in Yao, the precision
in Shun the compassionate
145　　in Yu the guider of waters

4 giants at the 4 corners
　　　three young men at the door
and they digged a ditch round about me
　　　lest the damp gnaw thru my bones
150　　　　　to redeem Zion with justice
sd/ Isaiah. Not out on interest said David rex
　　　　　　　　　　　　the prime s.o.b.
Light tensile immaculata
　　　　　　the sun's cord unspotted
155　" sunt lumina " said the Oirishman to King Carolus,
　　　　　　　　" OMNIA,
all things that are are lights "
and they dug him up out of sepulture
soi disantly looking for Manichaeans.
160　Les Albigeois, a problem of history,
and the fleet at Salamis made with money lent by the state to the
　　　　　　　　　　　　　　　　shipwrights
　　　　　　Tempus tacendi, tempus loquendi.
Never inside the country to raise the standard of living
165　but always abroad to increase the profits of usurers,
　　　　　　　dixit Lenin,
and gun sales lead to more gun sales
　　　they do not clutter the market for gunnery
　　　there is no saturation

170   Pisa, in the 23rd year of the effort in sight of the tower
    and Till was hung yesterday
      for murder and rape with trimmings   plus Cholkis
         plus mythology, thought he was Zeus ram or another one
            Hey Snag wots in the bibl'?
175   wot are the books ov the bible?
            Name 'em, don't bullshit ME.

莫   OΫ ΤΙΣ

a man on whom the sun has gone down
the ewe, he said had such a pretty look in her eyes;
180 and the nymph of the Hagoromo came to me,
                    as a corona of angels
one day were clouds banked on Taishan
      or in glory of sunset
           and tovarish blessed without aim
185 wept in the rainditch at evening
              Sunt lumina
that the drama is wholly subjective
stone knowing the form which the carver imparts it
the stone knows the form
190 sia Cythera, sia Ixotta, sia in Santa Maria dei Miracoli
    where Pietro Romano has fashioned the bases
OΫ ΤΙΣ
a man on whom the sun has gone down
nor shall diamond die in the avalanche
195   be it torn from its setting
first must destroy himself ere others destroy him.
4 times was the city rebuilded, Hooo Fasa
         Gassir, Hooo Fasa   dell' Italia tradita
now in the mind indestructible, Gassir, Hoooo Fasa,
200 With the four giants at the four corners
and four gates mid-wall Hooo Fasa
and a terrace the colour of stars
pale as the dawn cloud, la luna

thin as Demeter's hair
205 Hooo Fasa, and in a dance the renewal
with two larks in contrappunto
at sunset
ch'intenerisce
a sinistra la Torre
210 seen thru a pair of breeches.
Che sublia es laissa cader
between NEKUIA where are Alcmene and Tyro
and the Charybdis of action
to the solitude of Mt. Taishan
215 femina, femina, that wd/ not be dragged into paradise by the hair,
under the gray cliff in periplum
the sun dragging her stars
a man on whom the sun has gone down
and the wind came as hamadryas under the sun-beat
220 Vai soli
are never alone
amid the slaves learning slavery
and the dull driven back toward the jungle
are never alone 'HΛION ΠΕΡΙ 'HΛION
225 as the light sucks up vapor
and the tides follow Lucina
that had been a hard man in some ways
a day as a thousand years
as the leopard sat by his water dish;
230 hast killed the urochs and the bison sd/ Bunting
doing six months after that war was over
as pacifist tempted with chicken but declined to approve
of war " Redimiculum Metellorum "
privately printed
235 to the shame of various critics
nevertheless the state can lend money
and the fleet that went out to Salamis
was built by state loan to the builders

hence the attack on classical studies

240 and in this war were Joe Gould, Bunting and cummings
as against thickness and fatness

black that die in captivity
    night green of his pupil, as grape flesh and sea wave
undying luminous and translucent

245   Est consummatum, Ite;

      surrounded by herds and by cohorts looked on Mt Taishan

but in Tangier I saw from dead straw ignition
        From a snake bite
  fire came to the straw
250   from the fakir blowing
  foul straw and an arm-long snake
  that bit the tongue of the fakir making small holes
        and from the blood of the holes
          came fire when he stuffed the straw into his mouth
255 dirty straw that he took from the roadway
          first smoke and then the dull flame
  that wd/ have been in the time of Rais Uli
    when I rode out to Elson's
    near the villa of Perdicaris
260   or four years before that
elemental he thought the souls of the children, if any,
but had rented a shelter for travelers
  by foot from Siria, some of them
nor is it for nothing that the chrysalids mate in the air
265   color di luce
green splendour and as the sun thru pale fingers
Lordly men are to earth o'ergiven
    these the companions:
Fordie that wrote of giants

270   and William who dreamed of nobility
          and Jim the comedian singing:
              " Blarrney castle me darlin'
              you're nothing now but a StOWne "
      and Plarr talking of mathematics
275   or Jepson lover of jade
      Maurie who wrote historical novels
              and Newbolt who looked twice bathed
                  are to earth o'ergiven.
              And this day the sun was clouded
280   —" You sit stiller " said Kokka
      " if whenever you move something jangles."
      and the old Marchesa remembered a reception in Petersburg
      and Kokka thought there might be some society (good) left in
                  Spain, wd. he care to frequent it, my god, no!
285   opinion in 1924
      Sirdar, Bouiller and Les Lilas,
              or Dieudonné London, or Voisin's,
      Uncle George stood like a statesman 'PEI ΠΑΝΤΑ
      fills up every hollow
290   the cake shops in the Nevsky, and Schöners
      not to mention der Greif at Bolsano   la patronne getting older
      Mouquin's or Robert's 40 years after
          and La Marquise de Pierre had never before met an American
          " and all their generation "
295   no it is not in that chorus
          Huddy going out and taller than anyone present
                  où sont les heurs of that year
      Mr James shielding himself with Mrs Hawkesby
      as it were a bowl shielding itself with a walking stick
300   as he maneuvered his way toward the door
      Said Mr Adams, of the education,
              Teach? at Harvard?
              Teach? It cannot be done.
      and this I had from the monument

305   Haec sunt fastae
       Under Taishan quatorze Juillet
   with the hill ablaze north of Taishan
   and Amber Rives is dead, the end of that chapter
        see Time for June 25th,
310   Mr Graham himself unmistakeably,
      on a horse, an ear and the beard's point showing
     and the Farben works still intact
     to the tune of Lilibullero
   and they have bitched the Adelphi
315   niggers scaling the obstacle fence
       in the middle distance
   and Mr Edwards superb green and brown
       in ward No 4 a jacent benignity,
   of the Baluba mask: " doan you tell no one
320   I made you that table "
        methenamine eases the urine
   and the greatest is charity
   to be found among those who have not observed
        regulations
325   not of course that we advocate—
    and yet petty larceny
    in a regime based on grand larceny
    might rank as conformity nient' altro
    with justice shall be redeemed
330   who putteth not out his money on interest
    " in meteyard in weight or in measure "
       XIX Leviticus or
   First Thessalonians 4, 11
   300 years culture at the mercy of a tack hammer
335   thrown thru the roof
   Cloud over mountain, mountain over the cloud
   I surrender neither the empire nor the temples
         plural
   nor the constitution nor yet the city of Dioce

340   each one in his god's name
          as by Terracina rose from the sea Zephyr behind her
                    and from her manner of walking
                              as had Anchises
              till the shrine be again white with marble
345   till the stone eyes look again seaward
                              The wind is part of the process
                              The rain is part of the process
          and the Pleiades set in her mirror
          Kuanon, this stone bringeth sleep;
350   offered the wine bowl
                              grass nowhere out of place
          χθόνια γέα, Μήτηρ,
              by thy herbs menthe thyme and basilicum,
                  from whom and to whom,
355   will never be more now than at present
          being given a new green katydid of a Sunday
          emerald, paler than emerald,
                      minus its right propeller
                  this tent is to me and TIΘΩΝΩΙ
360   eater of grape pulp
                  in coitu inluminatio
          Manet painted the bar at La Cigale or at Les Folies in that year
                  she did her hair in small ringlets, à la 1880 it might have been,
          red, and the dress she wore Drecol or Lanvin
365   a great goddess, Aeneas knew her forthwith
          by paint immortal as no other age is immortal
                      la France dixneuvième
          Degas Manet Guys unforgettable
          a great brute sweating paint said Vanderpyl 40 years later
370   of Vlaminck
                  for this stone giveth sleep
                          staria senza più scosse
                  and eucalyptus that is for memory
                  under the olives, by cypress, mare Tirreno,

                                                          ■ 13

375   Past Malmaison in field by the river the tables
                 Sirdar, Armenonville
        Or at Ventadour the keys of the chateau;
                 rain, Ussel,
        To the left of la bella Torre   the tower of Ugolino
380   in the tower to the left of the tower
                 chewed his son's head
        and the only people who did anything of any interest were H., M.
                                                                 and
             Frobenius der Geheimrat
385   der im Baluba das Gewitter gemacht hat
                 and Monsieur Jean wrote a play now and then or the
                                                             Possum
             pouvrette et ancienne   oncques lettre ne lus
        I don't know how humanity stands it
390   with a painted paradise at the end of it
             without a painted paradise at the end of it
        the dwarf morning-glory twines round the grass blade
        magna NOX animae   with Barabbas and 2 thieves beside me,
                 the wards like a slave ship,
395   Mr Edwards, Hudson, Henry   *comes miseriae*
                     Comites Kernes, Green and Tom Wilson
                 God's messenger Whiteside
        and the guards op/ of the . . .
                 was lower than that of the prisoners
400   " all them g.d. m.f. generals c.s. all of 'em fascists "
        " fer a bag o' Dukes "
                         " the things I saye an' dooo "
             ac ego in harum
        so lay men in Circe's swine-sty;
405   ivi in harum *ego* ac vidi cadaveres animae
                 " c'mon small fry " sd/ the little coon to the big black;
        of the slaver as seen between decks
                 and all the presidents
        Washington Adams Monroe Polk Tyler

410   plus Carrol (of Carrolton) Crawford
     Robbing the public for private individual's gain ΘΕΛΓΕΙΝ
     every bank of discount is downright iniquity
         robbing the public for private individual's gain
         nec benecomata Kirkê, mah! κακὰ φάργακ' ἔδωκεν
415   neither with lions nor leopards attended
            but poison, veneno
     in all the veins of the commonweal
     if on high, will flow downward all thru them
         if on the forge at Predappio?   sd/ old Upward:
420   " not the priest but the victim "
         his seal Sitalkas, sd/ the old combattant: " victim,
     withstood them by Thames and by Niger with pistol by Niger
         with a printing press by the Thames bank"
         until I end my song
425   and shot himself;
                for praise of intaglios
     Matteo and Pisanello out of Babylon
            they are left us
     for roll or plain impact
430   or cut square in the jade block

     nox animae magna from the tent under Taishan
     amid what was termed the a.h. of the army
     the guards holding opinion. As it were to dream of
     morticians' daughters raddled but amorous
435   To study with the white wings of time passing
            is not that our delight
     to have friends come from far countries
            is not that pleasure
     nor to care that we are untrumpeted?
440   filial, fraternal affection is the root of humaneness
          the root of the process
     nor are elaborate speeches and slick alacrity.
         employ men in proper season

                    not when they are at harvest
445   E al Triedro, Cunizza
                e l'altra: " Io son' la Luna."
dry friable earth going from dust to more dust
        grass worn from its root-hold
        is it blacker? was it blacker? Nύξ animae?
450   is there a blacker or was it merely San Juan with a belly ache
                        writing ad posteros
        in short shall we look for a deeper or is this the bottom?
        Ugolino, the tower there on the tree line
Berlin   dysentery   phosphorus
455   la vieille de Candide
        (Hullo Corporal Casey) double X or burocracy?
                                Le Paradis n'est pas artificiel
        but spezzato apparently
it exists only in fragments unexpected excellent sausage,
460   the smell of mint, for example,
                    Ladro the night cat;
at Nemi waited on the slope above the lake sunken in the pocket
                                            of hills
awaiting decision from the old lunch cabin built out over the
465   shingle,
        Zarathustra, now desuete
        to Jupiter and to Hermes where now is the castellaro
                no vestige save in the air
        in stone is no imprint and the grey walls of no era
470   under the olives
                saeculorum Athenae
                γλαύξ, γλαυκῶπις,
                                    olivi
        that which gleams and then does not gleam
475   as the leaf turns in the air
                Boreas Apeliota libeccio
        " C'è il babao," said the young mother
                and the bathers like small birds under hawk's eye

16 ▪

shrank back under the cliff's edge at il Pozzetto
480   al Tigullio
" wd." said the guard " *take* everyone of them g.d.m.f. generals
c.s. all of 'em fascists "
            Oedipus, nepotes Remi magnanimi
so Mr Bullington lay on his back like an ape
485   singing: O sweet and lovely
o Lady be good "
                        in harum ac ego ivi
Criminals have no intellectual interests?
            and for three months did not know the taste of his food
490   in Chi heard Shun's music
                        the sharp song with sun under its radiance
                                    λιγύρ'
one tanka entitled the shadow
babao, or the hawk's wing
495   of no fortune and with a name to come
Is downright iniquity said J. Adams
                  at 35 instead of 21.65
                  doubtless conditioned by what his father heard in
                                                    Byzantium
500   doubtless conditioned by the spawn of the gt. Meyer Anselm
That old H. had heard from the ass eared militarist in Byzantium:
        " Why stop? " " To begin again when we are stronger."
and young H/ the tip from the augean stables in Paris
        with Sieff in attendance, or not
505   as the case may have been,
                                    thus conditioning.
Meyer Anselm, a rrromance, yes, yes certainly
but more fool you if you fall for it two centuries later
    . . .
510   from their seats the blond bastards, and cast 'em.
            the yidd is a stimulant, and the goyim are cattle
        in gt/ proportion and go to saleable slaughter
        with the maximum of docility.   but if

a place be versalzen,,,?
515   With justice,
by the law, from the law or it is not in the contract
      Yu has nothing pinned on Jehoveh
          sent and named Shun who to the
autumnal heavens *sha-o*
520   with the sun under its melody
      to the compassionate heavens
      and there is also the XIXth Leviticus.
      " Thou shalt purchase the field with money."
      signed Jeremiah
525   from the tower of Hananel unto Goah
unto the horse gate $8.50 in Anatoth
which is in Benjamin, $8.67
        For the purity of the air on Chocorua
        in a land of maple
530   From the law, by the law, so build yr/ temple
      with justice in meteyard and measure
a black delicate hand
a white's hand like a ham
      pass by, seen under the tent-flap
535   on sick call : comman'
        comman', sick call comman'
    and the two largest rackets are the alternation
      of the value of money
    (of the unit of money METATHEMENON TE TON
540   KRUMENON
and usury @ 60   or lending
      that which is made out of nothing
and the state *can* lend money   as was done
by Athens for the building of the Salamis fleet
545   and if the packet gets lost in transit
           ask Churchill's backers
    where it has got to   the state need not borrow
nor do the veterans need state guarantees

for private usurious lending
550   in fact that is the cat in the woodshed
the state need not borrow
as was shown by the mayor of Wörgl
who had a milk route
and whose wife sold shirts and short breeches
555   and on whose book-shelf was the Life of Henry Ford
and also a copy of the Divina Commedia
and of the Gedichte of Heine
a nice little town in the Tyrol in a wide flat-lying valley
near Innsbruck and when a note of the
560   small town of Wörgl went over
a counter in Innsbruck
and the banker saw it go over
all the slobs in Europe were terrified
" no one " said the Frau Burgomeister
565   " in this village who cd/ write a newspaper article.
Knew it was money but pretended it was not
in order to be on the safe side of the law."
But in Russia they bungled and did not apparently
grasp the idea of work-certificate
570   and started the N.E.P. with disaster
and the immolation of men to machinery
and the canal work and gt/ mortality
(which is as may be)
and went in for dumping in order to trouble the waters
575   in the usurers' hell-a-dice
all of which leads to the death-cells
each in the name of its god
or longevity because as says Aristotle
philosophy is not for young men
580   their *Katholou* can not be sufficiently derived from
their *hekasta*
their generalities cannot be born from a sufficient phalanx
of particulars

lord of his work and master of utterance
585   who turneth his word in its season and shapes it
          Yaou chose Shun to longevity
who seized the extremities and the opposites
holding true course between them
shielding men from their errors
590 cleaving to the good they had found
holding empire as if not in a mortar with it
          nor dazzled thereby
wd/ have put the old man, *son père* on his shoulders
      and gone off to some barren seacoast
595 Says the Japanese sentry : Paaak yu djeep over there,
some of the best soldiers we have says the captain
      Dai Nippon Banzai from the Philippines
remembering Kagekiyo : " how stiff the shaft of your neck is."
          and they went off each his own way .
600 " a better fencer than I was," said Kumasaka, a shade,
" I believe in the resurrection of Italy   quia impossibile est
     4 times to the song of Gassir
        now in the mind indestructible

             •   •   •   •

605   ΚΟΡΗ, ᾿ΑΓΛΑΟΣ ᾿ΑΛΑΟΥ
Glass-eye Wemyss treading water
      and addressing the carpenter from the seawaves
because of an unpinned section of taff-rail
     we are not so ignorant as you think in the navy
610 Gesell entered the Lindhauer government
which lasted rather less than 5 days
     but was acquitted as an innocent stranger
Oh yes, the money is there,
     il danaro c'è, said Pellegrini
615   (very peculiar under the circs)
     musketeers rather more than 20 years later
an old man (or oldish) still active

serving small stones from a lath racquet

Περσεφόνεια under Taishan

620   in sight of the tower che pende

on such a litter rode Pontius

         under such canvass

in the a.h. of the army

         in sight of two red cans labeled " FIRE "

625 Said Von Tirpitz to his daughter : beware of their charm

ΣΕΙΡΗΝΕΣ this cross turns with the sun

and the goyim are undoubtedly in great numbers cattle

whereas a jew will receive information

         he will gather up information

630   faute de...something more solid

            but not in all cases

ΣΕΙΡΗΝΕΣ   had appreciated his conversation

    ΧΑΡΙΤΕΣ possibly in the soft air

with the mast held by the left hand

635   in this air as of Kuanon

enigma forgetting the times and seasons

but this air brought her ashore a la marina

with the great shell borne on the seawaves

         nautilis biancastra

640   By no means an orderly Dantescan rising

but as the winds veer

            tira libeccio

now Genji at Suma   , tira libeccio

      as the winds veer and the raft is driven

645   and the voices   , Tiro, Alcmene

with you is Europa nec casta Pasiphaë

        Eurus, Apeliota as the winds veer in periplum

Io son la luna " . Cunizza

        as the winds veer in periplum

650   and from under the Rupe Tarpeia

drunk with wine of the Castelli

   " in the name of its god " " Spiritus veni "

adveni / not to a schema
        " is not for the young " said Arry, stagirite
655   but as grass under Zephyrus
            as the green blade under Apeliota
Time is not, Time is the evil, beloved
Beloved the hours βροδοδάκτυλος
            as against the half-light of the window
660   with the sea beyond making horizon
le contre-jour the line of the cameo
profile " to carve Achaia "
            a dream passing over the face in the half-light
            Venere, Cytherea " aut Rhodon "
665   vento ligure, veni
" beauty is difficult " sd/ Mr Beardsley
            and sd/ Mr Kettlewell looking up from a
pseudo-Beardsley of his freshman composition
    and speaking to W. Lawrence:
                            Pity you didn't finish the job
670
while you were at it "
            W.L. having run into the future non-sovereign Edvardus
on a bicycle equally freshman
                    a.d. 1910 or about that
675   beauty is difficult
in the days of the Berlin to Bagdad project
            and of Tom L's photos of rock temples in Arabia Petra
but he wd/ not talk of
            LL.G. and the frogbassador, he wanted to
680   talk modern art (T.L. did)
            but of second rate, not the first rate
            beauty is difficult.
He said I protested too much   he wanted to start a press
and print the greek classics....periplum
685   and the very *very* aged Snow created considerable
hilarity quoting the φαίνε-τ-τ-τ-τττ-αί μοι
in reply to *l'aer tremare*

                                beauty is difficult
                        But on the other hand the President of Magdalen
690   (rhyming dawdlin') said there were
            too many words in " The Hound of Heaven "
                            a moddddun opohem he had read
            and there was no doubt that the dons lived well

                                                    in the kawledg
695   it was if I remember rightly the burn and freeze that the fresh-

                                                                men
            had failed to follow
            or else a mere desire to titter etc.
            and it is (in parenthesis) doubtless
700   easier to teach them to roar like gorillas
            than to scan φαίνεταί μοι

                                    inferior gorillas
            of course, lacking the wind sack
                    and although Siki was quite observable
705   we have not yet calculated the sum   gorilla + bayonet
            and there was a good man named Burr
                        descendant of Aaron during the other war
            who was amused by the British
                        but he didn't last long AND
710   Corporal Casey tells me that Stalin
                        le bonhomme Staline
                        has no sense of humour (dear Koba!)
            and old Rhys, Ernest, was a lover of beauty
                        and when he was still engineer in a coal mine
715   a man passed him at high speed radiant in the mine gallery
            his face shining with ecstasy
                        " A'hv joost........Tommy Luff."
                        and as Luff was twice the fellow's size, Rhys was puzzled
            The Muses are daughters of memory
720   Clio, Terpsichore
            and Granville was a lover of beauty
            and the three ladies all waited

" and with a name to come "

εσσομένοισι

725   aram vult nemus

Came Madame Lucrezia
and on the back of the door in Cesena
are, or were, still the initials
joli quart d'heure, (nella Malatestiana)
730   Torquato where art thou?
to the click of hooves on the cobbles by Tevere
and " my fondest knight lie dead ".. or la Stuarda
" ghosts move about me " " patched with histories "
        but as Mead said: if they were,
735 *what have* they done in the interval,
      eh, to arrive by metempsychosis at....?
and there are also the conjectures of the Fortean Society
Beauty is difficult....the plain ground
          precedes the colours
740 and this grass or whatever here under the tentflaps
    is, indubitably, bambooiform
representative brush strokes wd/ be similar
....cheek bone, by verbal manifestation,
    her eyes as in " La Nascita "
745   whereas the child's face
is at Capoquadri in the fresco square over the doorway
    centre background
the form beached under Helios
      funge la purezza,
750 and that certain images be formed in the mind
      to remain there
        formato locho
  Arachne mi porta fortuna
to remain there, resurgent ΕΙΚΟΝΕΣ
755 and still in Trastevere

for the deification of emperors
and the medallions
                    to forge Achaia
and as for playing checquers with black Jim
760   on a barrel top where now is the Ritz-Carlton
and the voice of Monsieur Fouquet or the Napoleon 3rd
barbiche of Mr Quackenbos, or Quackenbush
as I supposed it,
and Mrs Chittenden's lofty air
765   and the remains of the old South
             tidewashed to Manhattan and brown-stone
             or (later) the outer front stair
leading to Mouquin's
        or old Train (Francis) on the pavement in his plain wooden
770   chair
or a fellow throwing a knife in the market
past baskets and bushels of peaches
                    at $1. the bushel
and the cool of the 42nd St. tunnel   (periplum)
775   white-wash and horse cars, the Lexington Avenue cable
refinement, pride of tradition, alabaster
                        Towers of Pisa
                        (alabaster, not ivory)
coloured photographs of Europa
780   carved wood from Venice venetian glass and the samovar
and the fire bucket, 1806 Barre Mass'chusetts
            and the Charter Oak in Connecticut
            or to begin with Cologne Cathedral
            the Torwaldsen lion and Paolo Uccello
785   and thence to Al Hambra, the lion court and el
            mirador de la reina Lindaraja
orient reaching to Tangier, the cliffs the villa of Perdicaris
Rais Uli, periplum
Mr Joyce also preoccupied with Gibraltar
790   and the Pillars of Hercules

■   25

not with my *patio* and the wistaria and the tennis courts
or the bugs in Mrs Jevons' hotel
  or the quality of the beer served to sailors
veder Nap'oiiiii or Pavia the romanesque
795   being preferable
and by analogy the form of San Zeno the
  columns signed by their maker
    the frescoes in S. Pietro and the madonna in Ortolo
e " fa di clarità l'aer tremare "
800 as in the manuscript of the Capitolare
Trattoria degli Apostoli (dodici)
" Ecco il tè " said the head waiter
in 1912 explaining its mysteries to the piccolo
with a teapot from another hotel
805 but coffee came to Assisi much later
    that is, so one cd/ drink it
when it was lost in Orleans and France semi-ruin'd
thus the coffee-house facts of Vienna
    whereas Mr Carver merits mention for the
810 cultivation of peanuts,
arachidi, and the soja has yet to save Europe
    and the wops do not use maple syrup
the useful operations of commerce
  stone after stone of beauty cast down
815 and authenticities disputed by parasites
    (made in Ragusa) and : what art do you handle?
" The best " And the moderns? " Oh, nothing modern
we couldn't sell anything modern."
But Herr Bacher's father made madonnas still in the tradition
820 carved wood as you might have found in any cathedral
   and another Bacher still cut intaglios
    such as Salustio's in the time of Ixotta,
where the masks come from, in the Tirol,
  in the winter season
825   searching every house to drive out the demons.

Serenely in the crystal jet
     as the bright ball that the fountain tosses
(Verlaine) as diamond clearness
     How soft the wind under Taishan
830   where the sea is remembered
     out of hell, the pit
     out of the dust and glare evil
     Zephyrus / Apeliota
This liquid is certainly a
835   property of the mind
nec accidens est   but an element
         in the mind's make-up
est agens and functions   dust to a fountain pan otherwise
     Hast 'ou seen the rose in the steel dust
840   (or swansdown ever?)
so light is the urging, so ordered the dark petals of iron
we who have passed over Lethe.

LXXV

Out of Phlegethon!
out of Phlegethon,
Gerhart
art thou come forth out of Phlegethon?
5 with Buxtehude and Klages in your satchel, with the
Ständebuch of Sachs in yr/ luggage
—not of one bird but of many

10

LXXVI

AND the sun high over horizon hidden in cloud bank
　　　lit saffron the cloud ridge
　　　　　　dove sta memora

" Will " said the Signora Agresti, " break his political
5　but not economic system "

But on the high cliff Alcmene,
　　　Dryas, Hamadryas ac Heliades
　　　flowered branch and sleeve moving
　　　Dirce et Ixotta e che fu chiamata Primavera
10　　　　　　in the timeless air

　　　that they suddenly stand in my room here
　　　between me and the olive tree
　　　　　or nel clivo ed al triedro?
　　　　　and answered : the sun in his great periplum
15　leads in his fleet here
　　　　　　sotto le nostre scogli
　　　under our craggy cliffs
　　　　　　alevel their mast-tops
　　　　　　Sigismundo by the Aurelia to Genova
20　　　　　　by la vecchia sotto S. Pantaleone
Cunizza qua al triedro,
e la scalza, and she who said: I still have the mould,
and the rain fell all the night long at Ussel
cette mauvaiseh venggg blew over Tolosa
25　and in Mt Segur there is wind space and rain space
　　　　　no more an altar to Mithras

from il triedro to the Castellaro

30　■

the olives grey over grey holding walls
and their leaves turn under Scirocco

30   la scalza : Io son' la luna
      and they have broken my house

the huntress in broken plaster keeps watch no longer

tempora, tempora and as to mores

by Babylonian wall (memorat Cheever)
35   out of his bas relief, for that line
we recall him
      and who's dead, and who isn't
      and will the world ever take up its course again?

very confidentially I ask you: Will it?
40   with Dieudonné dead and buried
not even a wall, or Mouquin, or Voisin or the cake shops
      in the Nevsky

      The Greif, yes, I suppose, and Schöners and perhaps
the Taverna and Robert's
45   but La Rupe no longer la Rupe, finito
Pré Catalan, Armenonville, Bullier
      extinct as Willy and there are I suppose
no reprints

Teofile's bricabrac Cocteau's bricabrac
50   seadrift snowin' 'em under
      every man to his junk-shop
houses shd/have been built in the '80's
(or '60's) for a' that
      but Eileen's trick sunlight softens London's November
55   progress, b . . . . h yr/progress

la pigrizia   to know the ground and the dew

but to keep 'em three weeks   Chung
                         we doubt it

and in government not to lie down on it
60   the word is made

perfect

better gift can no man make to a nation
          than the sense of Kung fu Tseu
                    who was called Chung Ni
65   nor in historiography nor in making anthologies

          (b . . . . h yr/progress)
          each one in the name of his god

So that in the synagogue in Gibraltar
          the sense of humour seemed to prevail
70   during the preliminary parts of the whatever
but they respected at least the scrolls of the law
               from it, by it, redemption
          @ $8.50, @ $8.67 buy the field with good money
no unrighteousness in meteyard or in measure (of prices)

75   and there is no need for the Xtns to pretend that
               they wrote Leviticus
               chapter XIX in particular
                    with justice Zion
          not by cheating the eye-teeth out of Don Fulano
80   or of Caio e Tizio;
          Why not rebuild it?

Criminals have no intellectual interests?
" Hey, Snag, wot are the books ov th' bibl' "

" name 'em, etc.
85   " Latin? I studied latin."
                said the nigger murderer to his cage-mate
            (cdn't be sure which of the two was speaking)
            " c'mon, small fry," sd/the smaller black lad
                        to the larger.
90   " Just playin' " ante mortem no scortum
            (that's progress, me yr' ' ' se/call it progress/)

        in the timeless air over the sea-cliffs
        " the pride of all our D.T.C. was pistol-packin' Burnes "
        But to set here the roads of France,
95   of Cahors, of Chalus,
                    the inn low by the river's edge,
        the poplars; to set here the roads of France
        Aubeterre, the quarried stone beyond Poitiers—
                    —as seen against Sergeant Beaucher's elegant profile—
100   and the tower on an almost triangular base
                    as seen from Santa Marta's in Tarascon

        " in heaven have I to make? "

                but all the vair and fair women
                and there is also the more northern (not nordic)
105   tradition from Memling to Elskamp, extending
                        to the ship models in Danzig...
        if they have not destroyed them
                    with Galla's rest, and...

        is measured by the *to whom* it happens
110   and to what, and if to a work of art
            then to all who have seen and who will not

        Washington, Adams, Tyler, Polk
            (with Crawford to bring in a few Colonial
                    families) the unruly

115   Tout dit que pas ne dure la fortune

           In fact a small rain storm...
                        as it were a mouse, out of cloud's mountain
                recalling the arrival of Joyce et fils
                        at the haunt of Catullus
120   with Jim's veneration of thunder and the
                Gardasee in magnificence
           But Miss Norton's memory for the conversation
                (or " go on ") of idiots
           was such as even the eminent Irish writer
125   has, if equalled at moments (? sintheticly)
                certainly never surpassed

                Tout dit que pas ne dure la fortune

           and the Canal Grande has lasted at least until our time
                even if Florian's has been refurbished
130   and shops in the Piazza kept up by
                        artificial respiration
           and for La Figlia di Jorio they got out a
                        special edition
                        (entitled the Oedipus of the Lagunes)
135   of caricatures of D'Annunzio

                        l'ara sul rostro
           20 years of the dream
                and the clouds near to Pisa
                        are as good as any in Italy
140   said the young Mozart: if you will take a *prise*
                or following Ponce (" Ponthe ")
                        to the fountain in Florida
           de Leon alla fuente florida
                or Anchises that laid hold of her flanks of air
145   drawing her to him
                        Cythera potens, Κύθηρα δεινά

no cloud, but the crystal body
      the tangent formed in the hand's cup
   as live wind in the beech grove
150   as strong air amid cypress

Κόρη, Δελιά δεινά/et libidinis expers
the sphere moving crystal, fluid,
     none therein carrying rancour
Death, insanity/suicide degeneration
155 that is, just getting stupider as they get older
πολλά παθεῖν,

                   nothing matters but the quality
of the affection—
in the end—that has carved the trace in the mind
160 dove sta memoria

and if theft be the main principle in government
      (every bank of discount J. Adams remarked)
there will be larceny on a minor pattern
a few camions, a stray packet of sugar
165   and the effect of the movies
       the guard did not think that the Führer had started it
Sergeant XL thought that excess population
         demanded slaughter at intervals
           (as to the by whom...) Known as ' The ripper.'

170   Lay in soft grass by the cliff's edge
with the sea 30 metres below this
       and at hand's span, at cubit's reach moving,
the crystalline, as inverse of water,
      clear over rock-bed

175   ac ferae familiares
the gemmed field *a destra* with fawn, with panther,

corn flower, thistle and sword-flower
to a half metre grass growth,
lay on the cliff's edge
180   ...nor is this yet *atasal*
nor are here souls, nec personae
neither here in hypostasis, this land is of Dione
and under her planet
to Helia the long meadow with poplars
185   to   Κύπρις
the mountain and shut garden of pear trees in flower
here rested.

      •   •   •   •

" both eyes, (the loss of) and to find someone
190   who talked his own dialect. We
talked of every boy and girl in the valley
but when he came back from leave
he was sad because he had been able to feel
all the ribs of his cow...."
195 this wind out of Carrara
is soft as *un terzo cielo*
              said the Prefetto
as the cat walked the porch rail at Gardone
the lake flowing away from that side
200 was still as is never in Sirmio
with Fujiyama above it: " La donna..."
            said the Prefect, in the silence

and the spring of their squeak-doll is broken
and Bracken is out and the B.B.C. can lie
205   but at least a different bilge will come out of it
       at least for a little, as is its nature
can continue, that is, to lie.

        As a lone ant from a broken ant-hill
from the wreckage of Europe, ego scriptor.

210   The rain has fallen, the wind coming down
     out of the mountain
     Lucca, Forti dei Marmi, Berchthold after the other one...
parts reassembled.
     ...and within the crystal, went up swift as Thetis
215   in colour rose-blue before sunset
and carmine and amber,

spiriti questi? personae?
       tangibility by no means *atasal*
       but the crystal can be weighed in the hand
220   formal and passing within the sphere: Thetis,
Maya, 'Αφροδίτη,

        no overstroke
     no dolphin faster in moving
       nor the flying azure of the wing'd fish under Zoagli
225   when he comes out into the air, living arrow.
and the clouds over the Pisan meadows
       are indubitably as fine as any to be seen
from the peninsula
       οἱ βάρβαροι have not destroyed them
230   as they have Sigismundo's Temple
    Divae Ixottae (and as to her effigy that was in Pisa?)
    Ladder at swing jump as for a descent from the cross
O white-chested martin, God damn it,
     as no one else will carry a message,
235   say to La Cara: amo.

Her bed-posts are of sapphire
     for this stone giveth sleep.

    and in spite of hoi barbaroi
    pervenche and a sort of dwarf morning-glory
240   that knots in the grass, and a sort of buttercup

et sequelae

Le Paradis n'est pas artificiel
    States of mind are inexplicable to us.
    δακρύων   δακρύων   δακρύων

245   L.   P.   gli onesti
              J'ai eu pitié des autres
probablement pas assez, and at moments that suited my own con-
                                   venience
          Le paradis n'est pas artificiel,
250   l'enfer non plus.

Came Eurus as comforter
and at sunset la pastorella dei suini
    driving the pigs home, benecomata dea

        under the two-winged cloud
255   as of less and more than a day
by the soap-smooth stone posts where San Vio
meets with il Canal Grande
between Salviati and the house that was of Don Carlos
shd/I chuck the lot into the tide-water?
260   le bozze " A Lume Spento "/
           and by the column of Todero
    shd/I shift to the other side
        or wait 24 hours,

        free then, therein the difference
265   in the great ghetto, left standing
with the new bridge of the Era where was the old eyesore
        Vendramin, Contrarini, Fonda, Fondecho
      and Tullio Romano carved the sirenes
        as the old custode says: so that since
270   then no one has been able to carve them
    for the jewel box, Santa Maria Dei Miracoli,

Dei Greci, San Giorgio, the place of skulls
                    in the Carpaccio
and in the font to the right as you enter
275   are all the gold domes of San Marco

Arachne, che mi porta fortuna, go spin on that tent rope

Unkle George in Brassitalo's abbazia
                    voi che passate per questa via:
                    Does D'Annunzio live here?
280   said the american lady, K. H.
              " I do not know " said the aged Veneziana,
                    " this lamp is for the virgin."
              " Non combaattere " said Giovanna,
              meaning: don't work so hard,

285   Arachne che mi porta fortuna;
                    Athene, who wrongs thee?
                    τίς ἀδικεῖ
       That butterfly has gone out thru my smoke hole

       Unkle George observing Ct/Volpe's neck at the Lido
290   and deducing his energy. Unkle G. stood like a statue
              " Rutherford Hayes on a monument "
                    as the princess approached him
              " You from New England? " barked the 10th District,

       and it came over me as he talked:
295   this is Dafne's Sandro—
              How? after 30 years,

       Trovaso, Gregorio, Vio

       " Dawnt let 'em git you " burred the bearded Dottore
       when was the Scottch Kirrrk in Venice

300   to warn one against Babylonian intrigue
      and there have been since then
 very high episcopal vagaries

    well, my window
   looked out on the Squero where Ogni Santi
305 meets San Trovaso
    things have ends and beginnings

 and the gilded cassoni neither then nor up to the present
 the hidden nest, Tami's dream, the great Ovid
    bound in thick boards, the bas relief of Ixotta
310   and the care in contriving
 Olim de Malatestis
        the long hall over the arches at Fano
 olim de Malatestis
      " 64 countries and down a boilin' volcano "
315   says the sargent
 ex rum-runner (the rum being vino rosso)
    " runnin whisky " sez he; mountain oysters?

    lisciate con lagrime
    politis lachrymis ΔΑΚΡΥΩΝ

320   bricks thought into being ex nihil
    suave in the cavity of the rock la concha
     ΠΟΙΚΙΛΟΘΡΟΝ', 'ΑΘΑΝΑΤΑ
      that butterfly has gone out thru my smoke hole
 'ΑΘΑΝΑΤΑ, saeva. Against buff the rose for the
325 background to Leonello, Petrus Pisani pinxit
    that a cameo should remain

 in Arezzo an altar fragment (Cortona, Angelico)
       po'eri di'aoli
 po'eri di'aoli sent to the slaughter

330   Knecht gegen Knecht
              to the sound of the bumm drum, to eat remnants
                   for a usurer's holiday to change the
          price of a currency
                        ΜΕΤΑΘΕΜΕΝΩΝ....
335   ΝΗΣΟΝ 'ΑΜΥΜΟΝΑ
              woe to them that conquer with armies
                   and whose only right is their power.

LXXVII

AND this day Abner lifted a shovel. . . . .
               instead of watchin' it to see if it would
          take action

Von Tirpitz said to his daughter..as we have elsewhere
5   recorded / he said: beware of their charm
               But on the other hand Maukch thought he
     would do me a favour by getting me onto the commission
     to inspect the mass graves at Katin,
               le beau monde gouverne
10   if not toujours at any rate it is a level of
     some sort whereto things tend to return
               Chung

               in the middle

     whether upright or horizontal
15   " and having got 'em (advantages, privilege)
     there is nothing, italics *nothing*, they will not do
     to retain 'em "
               yrs truly   Kungfutseu
     Entered the Bros Watson's store in Clinton N. Y.
20   preceded by a crash, i.e. by a
          huge gripsack or satchel
          which fell and skidded along the 20 foot aisle-way
          and ceased with a rumpus of glassware
               (unbreakable as it proved)
25   and with the enquiry: WOT IZZA COMIN'?

" I'll tell you wot izza comin'
               Sochy-lism is a-comin'

(a.d. 1904, somewhat previous but effective
for immediate scope

30   things have ends (or scopes) and beginnings.   To
know what precedes 先   and what follows 後

        will assist yr/ comprehension of process
        vide also Epictetus and Syrus

As Arcturus passes over my smoke-hole
35   the excess electric illumination
        is now focussed
on the bloke who stole a safe he cdn't open
            (interlude entitled: periplum by camion)
        and Awoi's *hennia*   plays hob in the tent flaps

40   k-lakk.....thuuuuuu
                making rain
                        uuuh
2,   7,   hooo
            der im Baluba

45   Faasa !   4 times was the city remade,
now in the heart indestructible
            4 gates, the 4 towers
(Il Scirocco è geloso)

                men rose out of χθόνος
50   Agada, Ganna, Silla,
    and Mt Taishan is faint as the wraith of my first friend
    who comes talking ceramics;
                mist glaze over mountain

    " How is it far, if you think of it? "

55   Came Boreas and his kylin
    to brreak the corporal's heart

Bright dawn 旦 on the sht house
    next day
      with the shadow of the gibbets attendant

60   The Pisan clouds are undoubtedly various
      and splendid as any I have seen since
at Scudder's Falls on the Schuylkill
    by which stream I seem to recall a feller
settin' in a rudimentary shack doin' nawthin'
65   not fishin', just watchin' the water,
    a man of about forty-five

    nothing counts save the quality of the affection

    mouth, is the sun that is god's mouth
or in another connection   (periplum)
70   the studio on the Regent's canal
    Theodora asleep on the sofa, the young
    Daimio's " tailor's bill "
    or Grishkin's photo refound years after
      with the feeling that Mr Eliot may have
75 missed something, after all, in composing his vignette
      periplum

(the dance is a medium)
    " To his native mountain "
    ψυχάριον ἀι βάσταζον νεκρὸν

80   a little flame for a little
conserved in the Imperial ballet, never danced in a theatre
Kept as Justinian left it
    Padre José had understood something or other
      before the deluxe car carried him over the precipice

85   *sumne fugol othbaer*
          learned what the Mass meant,
                    how one shd/ perform it

          the dancing at Corpus   the toys in the
                    service at Auxerre

90   top, whip, and the rest of them.

          [I heard it in the s.h.   a suitable place

          to hear that the war was over]

          the scollop of the sky shut down on its pearl
               καλλιπλόκαμα   Ida.
95   With drawn sword as at Nemi
                    day comes after day

          and the liars on the quai at Siracusa
                         still vie with Odysseus
          seven words to a bomb

100   dum capitolium scandet
               the rest is explodable
          Very potent, can they again put one together
          as the two halves of a seal, or a tally stick?

                         Shun's will and
105   King Wan's will

          were as the two halves of a seal
                    ½s
               in the Middle Kingdom

          Their aims as one
110   directio voluntatis, as lord over the heart
                    the two sages united

and Lord Byron lamented that he (Kung)
had not left it in metric
" halves of a seal,"

115   Voltaire choosing almost as I had
to finish his " Louis Quatorze "

and as to the distributive function
1766 ante Christum

it is recorded, and the state *can* lend money
120   as proved at Salamis
and for notes on monopoly
Thales;   and credit, Siena;
both for the trust and the mistrust;
" the earth belongs to the living "
125   interest on all it creates out of nothing
the buggering bank has;   pure iniquity
and to change the value of money, of the unit of
money
METATHEMENON
130   we are not yet out of *that* chapter
Le Paradis n'est pas artificiel
Κύθηρα,   Κύθηρα,
Moving ὑπὸ   χθονὸς   enters the hall of the records
the forms of men rose out of γέα
135   Le Paradis n'est pas artificiel
nor does the martin against the tempest
fly as in the calm air
" like an arrow, and under bad government
like an arrow "
140   " Missing the bull's eye seeks the cause in himself "
" only the total sincerity, the precise definition "
and no sow's ear from silk purse
even in that case...

the clouds over Pisa, over the two teats of Tellus, γέα

145 " He won't " said Pirandello " fall for Freud,
    he (Cocteau) is too good a poet."

Well, Campari is gone since that day
    with Dieudonné and with Voisin
and Gaudier's eye on the telluric mass of Miss Lowell

150 " the mind of Plato...   or that of Bacon "   said Upward
    seeking parallel for his own
" Haff you gno bolidigal basshunts?....
Demokritoos, Heragleitos " exclaimed Doktor Slonimsky 1912

So Miscio sat in the dark lacking the gasometer penny
155   but then said: " Do you speak German? "

   to Asquith, in 1914

" How Ainley face work all the time
        back of that mask "
But Mrs Tinkey never believed he wanted her cat
160 for mouse-chasing
    and not for oriental cuisine

" Jap'nese dance all time overcoat " he remarked
with perfect precision

" Just like Jack Dempsey's mitts " sang Mr Wilson

165   so that you cd/ crack a flea on eider wan
   ov her breasts
sd/ the old Dublin pilot
    or the precise definition

  bel seno (in rimas escarsas, vide sopra)

170   2 mountains with the Arno, I suppose, flowing between them
    so kissed the earth after sleeping on concrete

    bel seno Δημήτηρ copulatrix
          thy furrow

    in limbo no victories, there, are no victories—
175 that is limbo; between decks of the slaver
      10 years, 5 years

    " If he wd/ *only* get rid of Ciano " groaned the admiral
    " people who are used to take orders " he said
      when the fleet surrendered
180   " I would do it " (finish off Ciano) " with a pinch of
      insecticide."
      said Chilanti's 12 year old daughter.
  Sold the school-house at Gais,
  cut down the woods whose leaves served for bedding cattle
185   so there was a lack of manure...

    for losing the law of Chung Ni,
      hence the valise set by the alpino's statue in Brunik
      and the long lazy float of the banners
  and similar things occurred in Dalmatia
190   lacking that treasure of honesty
  which is the treasure of states
    and the dog-damn wop is not, save by exception,
  honest in administration any more than the briton is truthful

  Jactancy, vanity, peculation to the ruin of 20 years' labour

195 bells over Petano ...are softer than other bells
  remembering Alice and Edmée
    till the dog Arlechino makes his round
      blanket holding the hills' form in cloudy aurora

καὶ Ἴδα,   θέα   faces Apollo

200   E la Miranda was the only one who changed personality
                      changing her roles

      Which fact, it wd/ seem, escaped most, if not all, of the critics

      " If you had a f....n' brain you'd be dangerous "
                      remarks Romano Ramona
205   to a by him designated c.s. in the scabies ward
                      the army vocabulary contains almost 48 words
      one verb and participle one substantive   ὕλη
                      one adjective and one phrase sexless that is
      used as a sort of pronoun
210   from a watchman's club to a vamp or fair lady

      And Margherita's voice was clear as the notes of a clavichord
      tending her rabbit hutch,
                      O Margaret of the seven griefs
      who hast entered the lotus

215   " Trade, trade, trade.." sang Lanier
          and they say the gold her grandmother carried under her
      skirts for Jeff Davis
                drowned her when she slipped from the landing boat;
      doom of Atreus

220   (O Mercury god of thieves, your caduceus
          is now used by the american army
                      as witness this packing case)

      Born with Buddha's eye south of Mason and Dixon
      as against:
225   Ils n'existent pas, leur ambience leur confert
                      une existence...and in the case of

Emanuel Swedenborg...." do not argue "
                    in the 3rd sphere do not argue

above which, the lotus, white nenuphar
230   Kuanon, the mythologies

we who have passed over Lethe

            there are in fact several coarse expressions used in the
army and Monsieur Barzun had, indubitably, an idea, about anno

domini 1910 but I do not know what he has done with it
235   for I wd/ steal no man's raison
                    and old André
preached vers libre with Isaiaic fury, and sent me to old Rousselot
who fished for sound in the Seine
                    and led to detectors
240   " an animal " he said " which seeks to conceal the
            sound of its foot-steps "
                    L'Abbé Rousselot
who wrapped up De Sousa's poems (fin oreille)
and besought me to do likewise returning them
245   lest his housekeeper know that he had them.

" Un curé déguisé " sd/ Cocteau's of Maritain
        " Me parait un curé déguisé " A la porte
" Sais pas, Monsieur, il me parait un curé déguisé.

" Thought " said M. Cocteau   " that I was among men of letters
250   and then perceived a group of mechanics and garage assistants."
" As long as Daudet is alive they will never have him

    in the Académie Goncourt "
            sd/ La Comtesse de Rohan, and Mr Martin
we believe did a similar wrong to his party

255   " 30,000, they thought they were clever,
why, Hell / they cd/ have had it for 6000 dollars,
and after Landon they picked Wendell Willkie

              Roi je ne suis, prince je ne daigne
Citizen of Florence, cd/ not receive noble titles
260   but carry the arms to this day
who resisted at Arbia when the fools wd/ have burnt down
Florence " in gran dispitto "   " men used to obeying orders "
         " there was also the King who signed those decrees "
              se casco, non casco in ginocchion'

265   —niggers comin' over the obstacle fence
                   as in the insets at the Schifanoja
(del Cossa) to scale, 10,000 gibbet-iform posts supporting
              barbed wire
" St. Louis Till " as Green called him. Latin !
270   " I studied latin " said perhaps his smaller companion.
" Hey Snag, what's in the bibl' ?
              what are the books of the bibl' ?
Name 'em! don't bullshit me! "
         " Hobo Williams, the queen of them all "
275   " Hey / Crawford, come over here / "

                   Roma profugens Sabinorum in terras
" Sligo in heaven " murmured uncle William
              when the mist finally settled down on Tigullio

But Mr Joyce requested sample menus from the leading hotels
280   and Kitson had tinkered with lights on the Vetta

Mist covers the breasts of Tellus-Helena and drifts up the Arno
came night and with night the tempest
              " How is it far, if you think of it? "

If Basil sing of Shah Nameh, and wrote

فردوسی

285

Firdush' on his door

Thus saith Kabir: " Politically " said Rabindranath
          " they are inactive. They think, but then there is
climate, they think but it is warm or there are flies or
290 some insects "

" And with the return of the gold standard " wrote Sir Montagu
" every peasant had to pay twice as much grain
          to cover his taxes and interest "

It is true that the interest is now legally lower
295 but the banks lend to the bunya
who can thus lend more to his victims
and the snot press and periodical tosh does not notice this
thus saith Kabir, by hypostasis
if they can take Hancock's wharf they can take your cow
300   or my barn
and the Kohinoor and the rajah's emerald etc.

and Tom wore a tin disc, a circular can-lid
          with his name on it, solely:
for Wanjina has lost his mouth,

305   For nowt so much as a just peace
That wd/ obstruct future wars
as witness the bombardment at Frascati after the armistice
          had been signed

who live by debt and war profiteering
310   Das Bankgeschäft
               "....of the Wabash cannon ball "

52 ■

in flat Ferrarese country seemed the same as here under Taishan

men move to scale   as in Del Cossa's insets
          at Schifanoja under the Ram and Bull

315   in the house-boats bargaining half a day for ten bob's worth
            of turquoise

mind come to plenum when nothing more will go into it

the wind mad as Cassandra
       who was as sane as the lot of 'em

320   Sorella, mia sorella,
         che ballava sobr' un zecchin'

成   bringest to focus   成

ch'êng   *ch'êng*
        Zagreus

325   Zagreus

CANTO 77   Explication

中 — 1 - middle

先 — 2 - precede

後 — 3 - follow

何 — 4 - how (is it)

遠 — far

旦 — 5 - dawn

口 — 6 - mouth

非 — 7 - not

其 — one's own

鬼 — spirit

而 — and

祭 — sacrifice

之 — is

諂 — flattery

也 — bi gosh

To sacrifice to a spirit not one's own is flattery (sycophancy).

符 節 — 8 - halves of a
tally stick

496

志 — 9 - direction
of one's will

成 — 10 - perfect or
focus

LXXVIII

B Y THE square elm of Ida
    40 geese are assembled
    (little sister who could dance on a sax-pence)
    to arrange a pax mundi
5   *Sobr' un zecchin'!*
Cassandra, your eyes are like tigers,
    with no word written in them
You also have I carried to nowhere
    to an ill house and there is
10   no end to the journey.
        The chess board too lucid
the squares are too even...theatre of war...
" theatre " is good. There are those who did not want
    it to come to an end

15   and those negroes by the clothes-line are extraordinarily like the
        figures del Cossa
Their green does not swear at the landscape
2 months' life in 4 colours
    ter flebiliter: Ityn
20 to close the temple of Janus bifronte
    the two-faced bastard
" and the economic war has begun "
    Napoleon wath a goodth man, it took uth
    20 yearth to crwuth him
25 it will not take uth 20 years to crwuth Mussolini "
    as was remarked in via Balbo by the Imperial Chemicals
its brother.
    Firms failed as far off as Avignon...
...my red leather note-book

30   pax Medicea
        by his own talk in Naples, Lorenzo
            who left lyrics inoltre
            that men sing to this day
    " alla terra abbandonata "
35   followed him Metastasio;
    " alla " non " della " in il Programma di Verona
        the old hand as stylist still holding its cunning
    and the water flowing away from that side of the lake
    is silent as never at Sirmio
40   under the arches
    Foresteria, Salò, Gardone
            to dream the Republic. San Sepolchro
            the four bishops in metal

    lapped by the flame, amid ruin, la fede—
45   reliquaries seen on the altar.
    " Someone to take the blame if we slip up on it "
    Goedel's sleek head in the midst of it,
            the man out of Naxos past Fara Sabina
    " if you will stay for the night "
50   " it is true there is only one room for the lot of us "
    " money is nothing "
    " no, there is nothing to pay for that bread "
                    " nor for the minestra "
    " Nothing left here but women "
55   " Have lugged it this far, will keep it " (il zaino)
            No, they will do nothing to you.
    " Who says he is an American "
            a still form on the branda, Bologna
    " Gruss Gott," " Der Herr! " "Tatile ist gekommen! "
60   Slow lift of long banners
                Roma profugens Sabinorum in terras
    and belt the citye quahr of nobil fame
        the lateyn peopil taken has their name
    bringing his gods into Latium

65   saving the bricabrac
" Ere he his goddis brocht in Latio "
                " each one in the name "
in whom are the voices, keeping hand on the reins
Gaudier's word not blacked out

70   nor old Hulme's, nor Wyndham's,
Mana aboda.
The touch of sadism in the back of his neck
tinting justice, " Steele that is one awful name."
      sd/ the cheerful reflective nigger

75 Blood and Slaughter to help him
                  dialog repartee at the drain hole
Straight as the bar of a ducking stool " got his pride "
get to the states you can buy it
                  Don't try that here

80 the bearded owl making catcalls
                  Pallas Δίκη sustain me
" definition can not be shut down under a box lid "
but if the gelatine be effaced whereon is the record?
" wherein is no responsible person

85   having a front name, a hind name and an address "
" not a right but a duty "
            those words still stand uncancelled,
    " Presente! "
              and merrda for the monopolists

90   the bastardly lot of 'em
Put down the slave trade, made the desert to yield
and menaced the loan swine
             Sitalkas, double Sitalkas
             " not the priest but the victim "

95   said Allen Upward
knew something was phoney, when he (Pellegrini)
    sd/ : the money is there.
Knowledge lost with Justinian, and with Titus and Antoninus
  (" law rules the sea " meaning lex Rhodi)

100   that the state have vantage from private misfortune
No! Or the story of property
     to Rostovseff (is it Rostovseff?)
nothing worse than fixed charge
         several years' average
105   Mencius III, 1. T'ang Wan Kung
         Chapter 3 and verse 7
Be welcome, O cricket my grillo, but you must not
           sing after taps.
Guard's cap quattrocento
110   o-hon dit que'ke fois au vi'age
         qu'une casque ne sert pour rien
         'hien de tout
         Cela ne sert que pour donner courage
         a ceux qui n'en ont pas de tout
115   So Salzburg reopens
         Qui suona Wolfgang grillo
         P° viola da gamba
one might do worse than open a pub on Lake Garda
         so one thinks of
120   Tailhade and " Willy " (Gauthier-Villars)
         and of Mockel and La Wallonie...en casque
de crystal rose les baladines

         with the cakeshops in the Nevsky
and Sirdar, Armenonville or the Kashmiri house-boats
125   en casque de crystal rose les baladines
messed up Monsieur Mozart's house
         but left the door of the new concert hall
So he said, looking at the signed columns in San Zeno
" how the hell can we get any architecture
130   when we order our columns by the gross? "
red marble with a stone loop cast round it, four shafts,
and Farinata, kneeling in the cortile,
         built like Ubaldo, that's race,

Can Grande's grin like Tommy Cochran's
135   " E fa di clarità l'aer tremare "
                   thus writ, and conserved (or was) in Verona
So we sat there by the arena,
                       outside, Thiy and il decaduto
the lace cuff fallen over his knuckles
140   considering Rochefoucauld
but the program (Cafe Dante) a literary program 1920 or
               thereabouts was neither published nor followed
       Griffith said, years before that, : " Can't move 'em with
a cold thing like economics   I am pledged not to
145   come here (London) to Parliament "
                   Aram vult nemus
as under the rain altars
asking how to discover delusions (confusions)
                   " Chose Kao-yao and the crooks disappeared."
150   " Chose I Yin and the crooks toddled off."
                   2 hours of living, knew when they left
that there wd/ be one hell of a fight in the senate
                   Lodge, Knox against world entanglement
Two with him in the whole house against the constriction of
155   Bacchus
moved to repeal that god-damned amendment
                   Number XVIII
                           Mr Tinkham
Geneva the usurers' dunghill
160   Frogs, brits, with a few dutch pimps
as top dressing to preface extortions
                   and the usual filthiness
for detail see Odon's neat little volume
                   , that is, for a few of the more obvious details,
165   the root stench being usura and METATHEMENON
and Churchill's return to Midas broadcast by his liary.
                   " No longer necessary," taxes are no longer necessary
in the old way if it (money) be based on work done

inside a system and measured and gauged to human
170
requirements
inside the nation or system

道、

and cancelled in proportion

to what is used and worn out
à la Wörgl.   Sd/ one wd/ have to think about that
175
but was hang'd dead by the heels before his thought in proposito
came into action efficiently
" For a pig," Jepson said, " for a woman." For the infamies of
usura,
The Stealing of the Mare,   casûs bellorum,   " mits "
180
sang Mr Wilson, Thomas not Woodrow, Harriet's spirited heir
(the honours twice with his boots on,
that was Wellington)
and if theft be the main motive in government
in a large way
185
there will certainly be minor purloinments
As long as the socialists use their accessories as red herring
to keep man's mind off the creation of money
many men's mannirs   videt et urbes πολύμητις
ce rusé personnage, Otis,   so Nausikaa
190
took down the washing or at least went to see that the
maids didn't slack
or sat by the window
at Bagni Romagna   knowing that nothing could happen
and looking ironicly at the traveler
195
Cassandra your eyes are like tigers'
no light reaches through them
eating lotus, or if not exactly the lotus, the asphodel
To be gentildonna in a lost town in the mountains
on a balcony with an iron railing
200
with a servant behind her
as it might be in a play by Lope de Vega

and one goes by, not alone,
No hay amor sin celos

Sin segreto no hay amor

205
eyes of Doña Juana la loca,

Cunizza's shade al triedro and that presage
in the air

which means that nothing will happen that will
    be visible to the sargeants

210 Tre donne intorno alla mia mente

but as of conversation to follow,

boredom of that roman on Olivia's stairs
in her vision

that stone angle all of his scenery

215
with the balustrade, an antipodes

and as for the solidity of the white oxen in all this
    perhaps only Dr Williams (Bill Carlos)
will understand its importance,
    its benediction. He wd/ have put in the cart.

220 The shadow of the tent's peak treads on its corner peg

marking the hour. The moon split, no cloud nearer than Lucca.

In the spring and autumn
    In "The Spring and Autumn"
there

225
are
no
righteous
wars

LXXIX

M OON,   cloud,   tower,   a patch of the battistero
                                      all of a whiteness,
       dirt pile as per the Del Cossa inset
       think not that you wd/ gain if their least caress

5   were faded from my mind
I had not loved thee half so well
Loved I not womankind "
             So Salzburg reopens
         lit a flame in my thought that the years

10   Amari—li   Am——ar—i—li!
and her hair gone white   from the loss of him
           and she not yet thirty.
On her wedding day and then thus, for the next time,
           at the Spielhaus,

15   ...might have been two years later.
Or Astafieva inside the street doors of the Wigmore
               and wd/ not have known her
       undoubtedly wd/ have put in the cart)
present Mr G. Scott whistling Lili Marlene

20   with positively less musical talent
         than that of any other man of colour
             whom I have ever encountered
but with bonhomie and good humour
           (to Goedel in memoriam)

25   Sleek head that saved me out of one chaos
and I hear that G. P. has salmoned thru all of it.
Où sont? and who will come to the surface?
And Pétain not to be murdered   14 to 13
         after six hours' discussion

30   Indubitably, indubitably re/ Scott
         I like a certain number of shades in my landscape

as per / " doan' tell no one I made you that table "
or Whiteside:
                    " ah certainly dew lak dawgs,
35   ah goin' tuh wash you "
(no, not to the author, to the canine unwilling in question)
                    with 8 birds on a wire
or rather on 3 wires, Mr Allingham
The new Bechstein is electric
40   and the lark squawk has passed out of season
whereas the sight of a good nigger is cheering
        the bad'uns wont look you straight
Guard's cap quattrocento passes *a cavallo*
        on horseback thru landscape Cosimo Tura
45   or, as some think, Del Cossa;
up stream to delouse and down stream for the same purpose
seaward
different lice live in different waters
some minds take pleasure in counterpoint
50   pleasure in counterpoint
and the later Beethoven on the new Bechstein,
or in the Piazza S. Marco for example
finds a certain concordance of size
            not in the concert hall;
55   can that be the papal major sweatin' it out to the bumm drum?
what castrum romanum, what
                " went into winter quarters "
is under us?
as the young horse whinnies against the tubas
60   in contending for certain values
(Janequin per esempio, and Orazio Vechii or Bronzino)
Greek rascality against Hagoromo
        Kumasaka vs/ vulgarity
                no sooner out of Troas
65   than the damn fools attacked Ismarus of the Cicones
        4 birds on 3 wires, one bird on one

the imprint of the intaglio depends
     in part on what is pressed under it
the mould must hold what is poured into it

70   in
                  discourse
                        what matters is

to get it across e poi basta
          5 of 'em now on 2;
75   on 3; 7 on 4
                thus what's his name
     and the change in writing the song books
          5 on 3   aulentissima rosa fresca
so they have left the upper church at Assisi
80   but the Goncourt shed certain light on the
french revolution
          " paak you djeep oveh there "
the bacon-rind banner alias the Washington arms
            floats over against Ugolino
85 in San Stefano dei Cavalieri
            God bless the Constitution
and *save* it
          " the value thereof "
          that is the crux of the matter
90 and god damn the perverters
            and if Attlee attempts a Ramsey
" Leave the Duke, go for the gold "
            " in less than a geological epoch "
and the Fleet that triumphed at Salamis
95   and Wilkes's fixed the price per loaf
$\mathring{\eta}\theta os$
       Athene cd/ have done with more sex appeal
caesia oculi
" Pardon me, $\gamma\lambda\alpha\acute{v}\xi$ "
100   (" Leave it, I'm not a fool.")
mah?

        " The price is three altars, multa."
        " paak you djeep oveh there."

                    2 on 2

105   what's the name of that bastard? D'Arezzo, Gui d'Arezzo
        notation

             3 on 3
             chiacchierona   the yellow bird
        to rest   3 months in bottle
110   (auctor)
        by the two breasts of Tellus
           Bless my buttons, a staff car/
        si come avesse l'inferno in gran dispitto
        Capanaeus
115   with 6 on 3, swallow-tails
        as from the breasts of Helen, a cup of white gold
        2 cups for three altars. Tellus γέα feconda
          " each one in the name of its god "
          mint, thyme and basilicum,
120   the young horse whinnies against the sound of the bumm band;
        to that ' gadgett,' and to the production and the slaughter
        (on both sides) in memoriam
        " Hell! don't they get a break for the whistle? "
          and if the court be not the centre of learning...
125   in short the snot of pejorocracy...
                tinsel gilded
        of fat fussy old woman
          and fat snorty old stallions
          " half dead at the top "
130   My dear William B. Y. your ½ was too moderate
        " pragmatic pig " (if goyim) will serve for 2 thirds of it
        to say nothing of the investment of funds in the Yu-en-mi
        and similar ventures
          small arms 'n' chemicals
135   whereas Mr Keith comes nearest to Donatello's
          O Lynx, my love, my lovely lynx,

Keep watch over my wine pot,
Guard close my mountain still
Till the god come into this whiskey.
140   Manitou, god of lynxes, remember our corn.
Khardas, god of camels
                    what the deuce are you doing here?
I beg your pardon...
" Prepare to go on a journey."
145   " I..."

" Prepare to go on a journey."
or to count sheep in Phoenician,
                    How is it far if you think of it?
So they said to Lidya: no, your body-guard is not the
150   town executioner
the executioner is not here for the moment
the fellow who rides beside your coachman
            is just a cossak who executes...
            Which being the case, her holding dear H. J.
155   (Mr. James, Henry) literally by the button-hole...
in those so consecrated surroundings
                    (a garden in the Temple, no less)
                    and saying, *for once*, the right thing
namely: " Cher maître "
160   to his checqued waistcoat, the Princess Bariatinsky,
as the fish-tails said to Odysseus, ἐνὶ Τροίη,

            The moon has a swollen cheek
and when the morning sun lit up the shelves and battalions
of the West, cloud over cloud
165   Old Ez folded his blankets
Neither Eos nor Hesperus has suffered wrong at my hands

                    O Lynx, wake Silenus and Casey
                    shake the castagnettes of the bassarids,

the mountain forest is full of light
170   the tree-comb red-gilded
Who sleeps in the field of lynxes
            in the orchard of Maelids?
(with great blue marble eyes
            " because he likes to," the cossak)
175   Salazar, Scott, Dawley on sick call
            Polk, Tyler, half the presidents and Calhoun
" Retaliate on the capitalists " sd/ Calhoun " of the North "
ah yes, when the ideas were clearer
            debts to people in N. Y. city
180   and on the hill of the Maelids
in the close garden of Venus
            asleep amid serried lynxes
set wreathes on Priapus Ἴακχος, Io! Κύθηρα, Io!
            having root in the equities
185   Io!
            and you can make 5000 dollars a year
all you have to do is to make one trip up country
then come back to Shanghai
            and send in an annual report
190   as to the number of converts
            Sweetland on sick call
            ἐλέησον   Kyrie eleison
            each under his fig tree
            or with the smell of fig leaves burning
195   so shd/ be fire in winter
with fig wood, with cedar, and pine burrs

            O Lynx keep watch on my fire.

So Astafieva had conserved the tradition
From Byzance and before then
200   Manitou remember this fire
O lynx, keep the phylloxera from my grape vines

Ἴακχε, Ἴακχε, Χαῖρε, AOI
        " Eat of it not in the under world "
        See that the sun or the moon bless thy eating
205   Κόρη, Κόρη, for the six seeds of an error
or that the stars bless thy eating

        O Lynx, guard this orchard,
        Keep from Demeter's furrow

This fruit has a fire within it,
210   Pomona, Pomona
No glass is clearer than are the globes of this flame
what sea is clearer than the pomegranate body
        holding the flame?
           Pomona, Pomona,

215   Lynx, keep watch on this orchard
        That is named Melagrana
or the Pomegranate field
        The sea is not clearer in azure
        Nor the Heliads bringing light

220   Here are lynxes   Here are lynxes,
    Is there a sound in the forest
        of pard or of bassarid
    or crotale   or of leaves moving?

        Cythera, here are lynxes
225   Will the scrub-oak burst into flower?
    There is a rose vine in this underbrush
Red? white? No, but a colour between them
    When the pomegranate is open and the light falls
half thru it

230   Lynx, beware of these vine-thorns
        O Lynx, γλαυκῶπις coming up from the olive yards,

              Kuthera, here are Lynxes and the clicking of crotales
     There is a stir of dust from old leaves
        Will you trade roses for acorns
235   Will lynxes eat thorn leaves?
        What have you in that wine jar?
              ἰχώρ, for lynxes?

     Maelid and bassarid among lynxes;
          how many? There are more under the oak trees,
240   We are here waiting the sun-rise
        and the next sunrise
   for three nights amid lynxes. For three nights
     of the oak-wood
and the vines are thick in their branches
245   no vine lacking flower,
no lynx lacking a flower rope
      no Maelid minus a wine jar
this forest is named Melagrana

            O lynx, keep the edge on my cider
250   Keep it clear without cloud

We have lain here amid kalicanthus and sword-flower
      The heliads are caught in wild rose vine
The smell of pine mingles with rose leaves
        O lynx, be many
255   of spotted fur and sharp ears.
        O lynx, have your eyes gone yellow,
        with spotted fur and sharp ears?

     Therein is the dance of the bassarids
       Therein are centaurs
260   And now Priapus with Faunus
      The Graces have brought Ἀφροδίτην
      Her cell is drawn by ten leopards

                                      ■ 69

O lynx, guard my vineyard
As the grape swells under vine leaf
265 ʾΗλιος is come to our mountain
there is a red glow in the carpet of pine spikes

O lynx, guard my vineyard
As the grape swells under vine leaf

This Goddess was born of sea-foam
270 She is lighter than air under Hesperus
δεινὰ εἶ, Κύθηρα
terrible in resistance
Κόρη καὶ Δήλια καὶ Μαῖα
trine as praeludio
275 Κύπρις ᾿Αφρόδιτη
a petal lighter than sea-foam
Κύθηρα
aram
nemus
280 vult

O puma, sacred to Hermes, Cimbica servant of Helios.

LXXX

A IN' committed no federal crime,
           jes a slaight misdemeanor "
    Thus Mr A. Little or perhaps Mr Nelson, or Washington
    reflecting on the vagaries of our rising θέμις

5   Amo ergo sum, and in just that proportion
               And Margot's death will be counted the end of an era
       and dear Walter was sitting amid the spoils of Finlandia
       a good deal of polar white
               but the gas cut off.
10   Debussy preferred his playing
               that also was an era (Mr. W. Rummel)
       an era of croissants
               then an era of *pains au lait*
       and the eucalyptus bobble is missing
15   " Come pan, niño! "
       that was an era also, and Spanish bread
               was made out of grain in that era
               senesco
                       sed amo
20   Madri', Sevilla, Córdoba,
               there was grain equally in the bread of that era
               senesco sed amo
       Gervais must have put milk in his cheese
       (and the mortal fatigue of action postponed)
25   and Las Meniñas hung in a room by themselves
       and Philip horsed and not horsed and the dwarfs
                       and Don Juan of Austria
       Breda, the Virgin, Los Boracchos
                       are they all now in the Prado?
30   y Las Hilanderas?

Do they sell such old brass still in " Las Américas "
    with the wind coming hot off the marsh land
        or with death-chill from the mountains?
and with Symons remembering Verlaine at the Tabarin
35   or Hennique, Flaubert
Nothing but death, said Turgenev (Tiresias)
        is irreparable
ἀγλαὸς ἀλάου πόρνη Περσεφόνεια
    Still hath his mind entire
40   But to lose faith in a possible collaboration
To raise up the ivory wall
or to stand as the coral rises,
as the pilot-fish nears it
          (will they shoot X———y)
45   or the whale-mouth   for wanting a northern league
for demanding a Scandinavian Norse coalition
        inexorable
            this is from heaven
     the warp
50   and the woof
with a sky wet as ocean
flowing with liquid slate
Pétain defended Verdun while Blum
        was defending a bidet
55   the red and white stripes
        cut clearer against the slate
    than against any other distance
the blue field melts with the cloud-flow
To communicate and then stop, that is the
60   law of discourse
    To go far and come to an end
simplex munditiis, as the hair of Circe
perhaps without the munditiis
as the difference between the title page in old Legge
65 and some of the elegant fancy work

        I wonder what Tsu Tsze's calligraphy looked like
they say she could draw down birds from the trees,
      that indeed was imperial; but made hell in
the palace
70   as some say : a dark forest
                    the warp and the woof
                       that is of heaven
" and I be damned " said Confucius:
This affair of a southern Nancy
75   and as for the vagaries of our friend
                  Mr Hartmann,
Sadakichi a few more of him,
were that conceivable, would have enriched
        the life of Manhattan
80   or any other town or metropolis
the texts of his early stuff are probably lost
with the loss of fly-by-night periodicals
        and our knowledge of Hovey,
              Stickney, Loring,
85   the lost legion or as Santayana has said:
They just died   They died because they
       just couldn't stand it
and Carman " looked like a withered berry "
        20 years after
90   Whitman liked oysters
at least I think it was oysters
        and the clouds have made a pseudo-Vesuvius
             this side of Taishan
Nenni, Nenni, who will have the succession?
95   To this whiteness, Tseng said
       " What shall add to this whiteness? "
and as to poor old Benito
         one had a safety-pin
one had a bit of string, one had a button
100   all of them so far beneath him

half-baked and amateur
      or mere scoundrels
To sell their country for half a million
          hoping to cheat more out of the people
105   bought the place from the concierge
        who could not deliver
but on the other hand   emphasis
    an error or excess of
          emphasis
110   the problem after any revolution is what to do with
your gunmen
as old Billyum found out in Oireland
      in the Senate, Bedad! or before then
      Your gunmen thread on moi drreams
115   O woman shapely as a swan,
Your gunmen tread on my dreams
Whoi didn't he (Padraic Colum)
      keep on writing poetry at that voltage
" Whenever you get hold of one of their banknotes
120   (i.e. an Ulster note) burn it "
        said one of the senators
        planning the conquest of Ulster
This he said in the Oirish Senate
      showing a fine grasp of...
125   of possibly nothing,
If a man don't occasionally sit in a senate
      how can he pierce the darrk mind of a
            senator?

and down there they have been having their Palio
130   " Torre! Torre! Civetta! "
      and I trust they have not destroyed the
old theatre
        by restaurations, and by late renaissance giribizzi,
        dove è Barilli?

135   this calvario " we will not descend from," sd/ the *prete*
    on the damn'd hard bench waiting the horses
         and the parade and the carrocchio and the flag-play
    and the tossing of the flags of the contrade
        " for another four hours "
140   " non è una hontrada è un homplesso "
    explained an expert to an inexpert
    re/ the remains of the guilds or *arti*
    where they say: hamomila de hampo
        and the Osservanza is broken
145   and the best de la Robbia busted to flinders
        and near what? Li Saou
    and the front of the Tempio, Rimini
    It will not take uth twenty yearth
             to cwuth Mutholini
150   and the economic war has begun

                              35 via Balbo
    (Napoleon etc.) Since Waterloo
    nothing etc.   Leave the Duke, go for the gold!
    action somewhat sporadic
155   " Will never be used at home
            but abroad to increase the
    etc. of the lenders," the eh...investors
        and is buried in the Red Square in Mosqu
        along with Andy Jackson, Napoleon and others
160   there is according to some authors a partial resurrection
        of corpses
    on all souls day in Cairo
        or perhaps all over Egypt
        in identity but not atom for atom
165   but the Sadducees hardly give credence
    to Mr Eliot's version
    Partial resurrection in Cairo.
    Beddoes, I think, omits it.
        The bone *luz*, I think was his take off

170   Curious, is it not, that Mr Eliot
       has not given more time to Mr Beddoes
              (T. L.) prince of morticians
         where none can speak his language
    centuries hoarded
175   to pull up a mass of algae
              (and pearls)
    or the odour of eucalyptus or sea wrack
       cat-faced, croce di Malta, figura del sol
       to each tree its own mouth and savour
180   " *Hot*   *hole*   *hep*   *cat* "
    or words of similar volume
       to be recognized by the god-damned
           or man-damned trainee
    Prowling night-puss leave my hard squares alone
185   they are in no case cat food
           if you had sense
    you wd/ come here at meal time
         when meat is superabundant
    you can neither eat manuscript nor Confucius
190   nor even the hebrew scriptures
       get out of that bacon box
       contract W, 11 oh oh 9 oh
    now used as a wardrobe
             ex 53 pounds gross weight
195   the cat-faced eucalyptus nib
         is where you cannot get at it
       Tune: kitten on the keys
         radio steam Calliope
    following the Battle Hymn of the Republic
200   where the honey-wagon cease from stinking
               and the nose be at peace
  " mi-hine eyes hev "
            well yes they *have*
  seen a good deal of it

何
遠

205   there is a good deal to be seen
fairly tough and unblastable
            and the hymn...
well in contrast to the *god*-damned crooning
        put me down for temporis acti
210   OΥ ΤΙΣ
          ἄχρονος
now there are no more days
          οὔ τις
          ἄχρονος
215   the water seeps in under the bottle's seal
                Till finally the moon rose like a blue p.c.
of Bingen on the Rhine
                round as Perkeo's tub
then glaring Eos stared the moon in the face
220   (Pistol packin' Jones with an olive branch)   *ch'üan*³
        man and dog
                    on the S. E. horizon
            and we note that dog precedes man in the occident
            as of course in the orient if the bloke in the
225   is proceeding to rightwards
        " Why war? " sd/ the sergeant rum-runner
        " too many people! when there git to be too many
                    you got to kill some of 'em off."
" But for Kuan Chung," sd/ Confucius
230   " we shd / still be buttoning our coats tother way on."
the level of political education in our
eminent armies
        is, perhaps, not yet established   ma
così discesi per l'aer maligno
235   on doit le temps ainsi prendre qu'il vient
or to write dialog because there is
                no one to converse with
to take the sheep out to pasture
to bring your g.r. to the nutriment

240   gentle reader   to the gist of the discourse
               to sort out the animals

       so that leaving America I brought with me $80
          and England a letter of Thomas Hardy's
          and Italy one eucalyptus pip
245   from the salita that goes up from Rapallo
                 (if I go)
" a S. Bartolomeo mi vidi col pargoletto,
Chiodato a terra colle braccie aperte
                 in forma di croce gemisti.
250   disse: Io son' la luna."
Coi piedi sulla falce d'argento
         mi parve di pietosa sembianza
The young Dumas weeps because the young Dumas
has tears
255   Death's seeds move in the year
                   semina motuum
        falling back into the trough of the sea
         the moon's arse been chewed off by this time
semina motuum
260   " With us there is no deceit "
          said the moon nymph   immacolata
          Give back my cloak, *hagoromo.*
          had I the clouds of heaven
             as the nautile borne ashore
265   in their holocaust
            as wistaria floating shoreward
with the sea gone the colour of copper
       and emerald dark in the offing
the young Dumas has tears thus far from the year's end
270 At Ephesus she had compassion on silversmiths

revealing the paraclete
standing in the cusp
    of the moon et in Monte Gioiosa
    as the larks rise at Allegre
275   Cythera egoista
    But for Actaeon
    of the eternal moods has fallen away
in Fano Caesaris for the long room over the arches
olim de Malatestis

280   wan   caritas   ΧΑΡΙΤΕΣ

and when bad government prevailed, like an arrow,
fog rose from the marshland
        bringing claustrophobia of the mist
beyond the stockade there is chaos and nothingness
285   Ade du Piccadilly
               Ade du Lesterplatz
Their works like cobwebs when the spider is gone
    encrust them with sun-shot crystals
and in 40 years no one save old Bellotti
290   " There is no darkness but ignorance "
    had read the words on the pedestal
The things I cd/ tell you, he sd/ of Lady de X
and of how he caught the Caressor's about to be
        Imperial coat tails
295 and only twice had rec'd 3 penny bits
        one from Rothschild and one from DeLara
and brought in about 2 ounces of saffron
for a risotto during that first so enormous war
        Jah, the Bard's pedestal ist am Lesterplatz
300 in the city of London
but the trope is, as the accurate reader will have observed,
not to be found in Sam Johnson's edition
The evil that men do lives after them "

well, that is from Julius Caesar
305   unless memory trick me
who crossed the Rubicon up near Rimini
Where is, or was, an arch of Augustus
            " Wanted to borrow it back " said H. Cole
            " I sd/ why? he thought he wd/
310   make another one like it " so Horace C. started
buying someone else's paintings
                whose name, be it not Innes, escapes me
But impersonated a sultan
of was it Zanzibar and took up the paving in Bond St.
315   to compensate for a partial deafness
which, he felt, lost him part of life's fun
and persuaded an Aussie or Zealander or S. African
to kneel with him in prayer
                outside the Kardomah tea rooms
320   and also roused a street demonstration
            in Soho for Italy's entry into combat in
                19 was it 15?
pass Napper, Bottom (correct that to Bottomly)
                Gaddy on sick call

325   will be wanted for gunstocks or need belladonna
                and as for sulking
I knew but one Achilles in my time
and he ended up in the Vatican
                Hannibals, Hamilcars
330   in profusion nearly all humble persons
" Jolly woman " said the resplendent head waiter
20 years after i.e. after old Kait'
had puffed in, stewing with rage
concerning the landlady's *doings*
335   with a lodger unnamed
az waz near Gt Tichfield St. next door to the pub
" married wumman, you couldn't fool *her* "
Torn from the *sacerdos*

80 ▪

<pre>
                    hurled into unstillness, Ixion
340   Trinacrian manxman
                      So old Sauter
       front hall full of large photos of Bismark
              and Von Moltke
       so that during the Boer war Whistler used to come
345   and talk strategy
                           but that he, Sauter, never cd/ see
       the portrait of Sarasate
              " like a black fly hanging stuck to that canvas "
       till one day after Whistler's death
350   I think it was Ysaÿe was with him
                      who saw the Whistler
       for the first time and burst out:
                                    What a fiddle!

       It is said also that Homer was a medic
355   who followed the greek armies to Troas
       so in Holland Park they rolled out to beat up Mr Leber
       (restaurantier) to Monsieur Dulac's disgust
       and a navvy rolls up to me in Church St. (Kensington End) with:
                      Yurra Jurrmun!
360   To which I replied: I am not.
       " Well yurr szum kind ov a furriner."
                      ne povans desraciner
       But Tosch the great ex-greyhound
              used to get wildly excited
365   at being given large beefsteaks
       in Tolosa
                      and leapt one day finally
       right into the centre of the large dining table
       and lay there as a centre piece
370   near the cupboard piled half full
       with novels of " Willy " etc
                      in the old one franc editions
</pre>

and you cd/ hear papa Dulac's voice
    clear in the choir that wd/ ring ping on the high altar
375   in the Bach chorals
        true as a pistol shot
and he dumped all his old stock
    of calicos plumb bang on the germans
after two or more years of stagnation
380   it was at Leber's that old Colonel Jackson
had said to Gaudier:
                " mes compliments "
when Gaudier had said he wd/ fight for la Patrie if war came
but that anarchy was the true form of government
385   (meaning, so far as I cd/ make out, some form of
        sindical organization
Jackson at 80 proposed to cook for the armies of Ulster
    " la bonne soupe fait le bon soldat ")
    and he said to Yeats at a vorticist picture show:
390   " You also of the brotherhood? "
But Dolmetsch died without ever knowing that Dulac
    had broken and mended the support to the lid
of one of his clavichords, Dolmetsch' own clavichords
    painted and toned with that special sacred vermilion,
395   " Il est bon comme le pain "
                sd/ Mockel of " Willy "
(Gauthier Villars) but I cdn't explain to him (Willy)
what the Dial wanted and Gluck's " Iphigénie "
    was played in the Mockel's garden
400   Les mœurs passent et la douleur reste.
" En casque de crystal rose les baladines "
    Mallarmé, Whistler, Charles Condor, Degas
and the bar of the Follies
        as Manet saw it, Degas, those two gents crossing ' La
405   Concorde ' or for that matter
Judith's junk shop
        with Théophile's arm chair

one cd/ live in such an apartment
seeing the roofs of Paris
410   Ça s'appelle une mansarde
The old trees near the Rue Jacob
                    were propped up to keep them from falling
à l'Amitié
and M. Jean wanted to save that building
415   what do you call it,
can it have been the old École Militaire?
    " Il me paraît," said his housekeeper
                        " un curé déguisé "
(that was Maritain)
420   and Natalie said to the apache:
                    vous êtes très mal élevé
        and his companion said: Tiens, elle te le dit...
            so they left her her hand bag
and the jambe-de-bois stuck it up
425   at an angle, say about 140 degrees
        and pretended it was a fiddle
            while the 60 year old bat did a hoolah
        to the great applause of that bistro
                " Entrez donc, mais entrez,
430   c'est la maison de tout le monde "
(This to me and H. Liveright vers le Noël)
And three small boys on three bicycles
            smacked her young fanny in passing
before she recovered from the surprise of the first swat
435   ce sont les mœurs de Lutèce
            where there are also the scant remains of an arena
and Le Musée de Cluny.
            Arena or is it a teatro romano?
and there was also Uncle William
440   labouring a sonnet of Ronsard
and the ink's heir painting high lights
        and Monsieur C. who paid, I think, bills for La Falange

and M. Arnold Bennett etc
" Ah Monsieur " said old Carolus (Durand)
445   " vous allez raser une toile? "
and after Puvis had come Carrière
                         (o-hon dit quelque fois au vi'age)
when they elected old Brisset Prince des Penseurs,
              Romains, Vildrac and Chennevière and the rest of them
450   before the world was given over to wars
              Quand vous serez bien vieille
                    remember that I have remembered,
mia pargoletta,
          and pass on the tradition
455   there can be honesty of mind
                    without overwhelming talent
I have perhaps seen a waning of that tradition
(young nigger at rest in his wheelbarrow
          in the shade back of the jo-house
460   addresses me: Got it *made,* kid, you got it made.
White boy says: do you speak Jugoslavian?)
And also near the museum they served it mit Schlag
          in those days (pre 1914)
          the loss of that café
465   meant the end of a B. M. era
                    (British Museum era)
Mr Lewis had been to Spain
          Mr Binyon's young prodigies
pronounced the word: Penthesilea
470   There were mysterious figures
that emerged from recondite recesses
              and ate at the WIENER CAFÉ
which died into banking, Jozefff may have followed
his emperor.
475   " It is the sons pent up within a man "
mumbled old Neptune
                    " Laomedon, Ahi, Laomedon "

or rather three " ahis " before the " Laomedon "
    " He stood " wrote Mr Newbolt, later Sir Henry,
480   " the door behind " and now they complain of cummings.
So it is to Mr Binyon that I owe, initially,
Mr Lewis, Mr P. Wyndham Lewis. His bull-dog, me,
    as it were against old Sturge M's bull-dog, Mr T. Sturge Moore's
       bull-dog, et
485   meum est propositum, it is my intention
in tabernam, or was, to the Wiener café
you cannot yet buy one dish of Chinese food in all Italy
hence the débacle
" forloyn " said Mr Bridges (Robert)
490   " we'll get 'em all back "
meaning archaic words and there had been a fine old fellow
named Furnivall and Dr. Weir Mitchell collected

And the Franklin Inn club...
    and young fellows go out to the colonies
495   but go on paying their dues
but old William was right in contending
    that the crumbling of a fine house
profits no one
    (Celtic or otherwise)
500   nor under Gesell would it happen

As Mabel's red head was a fine sight
worthy his minstrelsy
a tongue to the sea-cliffs or " Sligo in Heaven "
or his, William's, old " da " at Coney Island perched on an elephant
505   beaming like the prophet Isaiah
    and J. Q. as it were aged 8 (Mr John Quinn)
at the target.

    " Liquids and fluids! "
    said the palmist. " A painter?

510 well ain't that liquids and fluids? " [To the venerable J. B.
          bearded Yeats]

      " a friend," sd/ mr cummings, " I knew it 'cause he
      never tried to sell *me* any insurance "

      (with memorial to Warren Dahler the Chris Columbus of
515   Patchin)

      Hier wohnt the tradition, as per Whitman in Camden
      and an engraving 596 Lexington Ave.,
                          24 E. 47th,
      with Jim at the checquer board by the banana cage

520 " Funny looking wood, James," said Aunt F.
      " it looks as if it had already been burnt "
                                          [Windsor fire]
              " Part o deh roof ma'am."
              does any museum
525 contain one of the folding beds of that era?
      And now, why?   Regents Park
              where was the maison Alma-Tadema
              (with a fountain) or Leighton House
                              for that matter?
530 and the mass of preraphaelite reliques
              in a trunk in a walled-up cellar in Selsey
      " Tyke 'im up ter the bawth " (meaning Swinburne)
      " Even Tennyson tried to go out
          through the fire-place."

535 which is what I suppose he, Fordie, wanted me to be able to picture
      when he took me to Miss Braddon's
          (I mean the setting) at Richmond
      But that New York I have found at Périgueux
                          si com' ad Arli

540 in wake of the sarascen
     As the " Surrender of Breda " (Velásquez)
 was preceded in fresco at Avignon
   y cavals armatz with the perpendicular lances
 and the red-bearded fellow was mending his
545   young daughter's shoe
 " Me Hercule! c'est nôtre comune "
 (" Borr," not precisely Altaforte)
   with such dignity
 and at Ventadour and at Aubeterre
550 or where they set tables down by small rivers,
 and the stream's edge is lost in grass
    (Unkle George cd/ not identify the place on that road
 because the road had been blown off the side of the mountain
 but he climbed about 200 steps of the tower
555 to see what he had seen thru the roof
   of a barn no longer standing
        sul Piave
 where he had fired that howitzer
 and the large eye that found him
560 at its level was a giraffe's eye
    at dawn, in his nest, hunting leopards.

 " The pose " he said " is a taxidermist's fake
    the cobra is not a constrictor
 and would not wrap itself round the mongoose "
565 But on the subject of terrapin
    would not believe they cd/ fly
      and the bishop brought action for libel
 (I think half a million but did not, finally,
        take the case into court)

570 by which time Uncle George was computing
    Volpe's kilowatt energy
 from the back of his neck as seen at the Lido Excelsior

and in that year at Florian's Sir Ronald
had said: the Negus is not a bad fellowe.
575   In fact the milk-white doe for his cousin
                reminding me of the Bank of Egypt
                        and the gold bars
in old Menelik's palace and the mahogany counters
and desk work in the branch in, was it, Alessandria
580   put there by Pea (Enrico)

and wd/ Whitcomb Riley be still found in a highbrow anthology

                Nancy where art thou?
Whither go all the vair and the cisclatons
and the wave pattern runs in the stone
585   on the high parapet (Excideuil)
Mt Segur and the city of Dioce
Que tous les mois avons nouvelle lune
What the deuce has Herbiet (Christian)
                done with his painting?
590   Fritz still roaring at treize rue Gay de Lussac
with his stone head still on the balcony?
Orage, Fordie, Crevel too quickly taken

                de mis soledades vengan

lay there till Rossetti found it remaindered
595   at about two pence
        (Cythera, in the moon's barge whither?
                how hast thou the crescent for car?

or did they fall because of their loose taste in music
        " Here! none of that mathematical music! "
600   Said the Kommandant when Münch offered Bach to the regiment
or Spewcini the all too human
                beloved in the eyetalian peninsula

for quite explicable reasons
    so that even I can now tolerate
605   man seht but with the loss of criteria
and the wandering almost-tenor explained to me:
        well, the operas in the usual repertoire
have been sifted out, there's a reason

Les hommes ont je ne sais quelle peur étrange,
610   said Monsieur Whoosis, de la beauté

La beauté, " Beauty is difficult, Yeats " said Aubrey Beardsley
    when Yeats asked why he drew horrors
    or at least not Burne-Jones
    and Beardsley knew he was dying and had to
615   make his hit quickly

hence no more B-J in his product.

So very difficult, Yeats, beauty so difficult.

" I am the torch " wrote Arthur " she saith "
in the moon barge βροδοδάκτυλος Ἠώς

620   with the veil of faint cloud before her
        Κύθηρα δεινὰ as a leaf borne in the current
pale eyes as if without fire

all that Sandro knew, and Jacopo
        and that Velásquez never suspected
625   lost in the brown meat of Rembrandt
        and the raw meat of Rubens and Jordaens

" This alone, leather and bones between you and τὸ πᾶν,"
                  [toh pan, the all]
      (Chu Hsi's comment)

630   or the bone *luz*
        as the grain seed and the biceps
                books, arms, men, as with Sigismundo

        and of portraits in our time Cocteau by Marie Laurencin
        and Whistler's Miss Alexander
635   (and the three fat ladies by Sargent, adversely)
                and somebody's portrait of Rodenbach
                        with a background
        as it might be L'Ile St Louis for serenity, under Abélard's bridges
        for those trees are Elysium
640   for serenity
                        under Abélard's bridges   πάντα ʿρεῖ
        for those trees are serenity

        as he had walked under the rain altars
                or under the trees of their grove
645   or would it be under their parapets
        in his moving was stillness
        as grey stone in the Aliscans
                or had been at Mt Segur
        and it was old Spencer (, H.) who first declaimed me the Odyssey
650   with a head built like Bill Shepard's
        on the quais of what Siracusa?
                or what tennis court
        near what pine trees?

        care and craft in forming leagues and alliances
655   that avail nothing against the decree
        the folly of attacking that island
                and of the force ὑπὲρ μόρον

        with a mind like that he is one of us
                Favonus, vento benigno
660   Je suis au bout de mes forces/

That from the gates of death,
>   that from the gates of death: Whitman or Lovelace
>   found on the jo-house seat at that
in a cheap edition! [and thanks to Professor Speare]
665   hast'ou swum in a sea of air strip
>   through an aeon of nothingness,
when the raft broke and the waters went over me,

Immaculata, Introibo
>   for those who drink of the bitterness
670   Perpetua, Agatha, Anastasia
>   saeculorum

repos donnez à cils
>   senza termine funge   Immaculata Regina
>   Les larmes que j'ai creées m'inondent
675   Tard, très tard je t'ai connue, la Tristesse,
I have been hard as youth sixty years

>   if calm be after tempest
that the ants seem to wobble
>   as the morning sun catches their shadows
680   (Nadasky, Duett, McAllister,
>   also Comfort K.P. special mention
>   on sick call Penrieth, Turner, Toth hieri
>   (no fortune and with a name to come)
Bankers, Seitz, Hildebrand and Cornelison
685   Armstrong special mention K.P.
>   White gratia Bedell gratia
>   Wiseman (not William) africanus.
with a smoky torch thru the unending
>   labyrinth of the souterrain
690   or remembering Carleton let him celebrate Christ in the grain
and if the corn cat be beaten
>   Demeter has lain in my furrow

This wind is lighter than swansdown
    the day moves not at all
695   (Zupp, Bufford, and Bohon)

men of no fortune and with a name to come

his helmet is used for a pisspot
this helmet is used for my footbath
    Elpenor can count the shingle under Zoagli
700   Pepitone was wasting toothwash
       as I lay by the drain hole
the guard's opinion is lower than that of the
    prisoners

        o.   t.   a.

705   Oh to be in England now that Winston's out
       Now that there's room for doubt
           And the bank may be the nation's
           And the long years of patience
           And labour's vacillations
710   May have let the bacon come home,
               To watch how they'll slip and slide
               watch how they'll try to hide
                  the real portent
        To watch a while from the tower
715   where dead flies lie thick over the old charter
       forgotten, oh quite forgotten
         but confirming John's first one,
     and still there if you climb over attic rafters;
   to look at the fields; are they tilled?
720 is the old terrace alive as it might be
with a whole colony
           if money be free again?

Chesterton's England of has-been and why-not,
or is it all rust, ruin, death duties and mortgages
725   and the great carriage yard empty
                    and more pictures gone to pay taxes

        When a dog is tall but
        not so tall as all that
        that dog is a Talbot
730   (a bit long in the pasterns?)
When a butt is ½ as tall as a whole butt
That butt is a small butt
            Let backe and side go bare
and the old kitchen left as the monks had left it
735   and the rest as time has cleft it.

[Only shadows enter my tent
                as men pass between me and the sunset,]
beyond the eastern barbed wire
        a sow with nine boneen
740   matronly as any duchess at Claridge's

and for that Christmas at Maurie Hewlett's
Going out from Southampton
they passed the car by the dozen
        who would not have shown weight on a scale
745   riding, riding
                        for Noel the green holly
        Noel, Noel, the green holly
        A dark night for the holly

That would have been Salisbury plain, and I have not thought of
750   the Lady Anne for this twelve years
                Nor of Le Portel
How tiny the panelled room where they stabbed him
            In her lap, almost, La Stuarda

                   Si tuit li dolh ehl planh el marrimen
755   for the leopards and broom plants

         Tudor indeed is gone and every rose,
         Blood-red, blanch-white that in the sunset glows
         Cries: " Blood,   Blood,   Blood! " against the gothic stone
         Of England, as the Howard or Boleyn knows.

760   Nor seeks the carmine petal to infer;
         Nor is the white bud Time's inquisitor
         Probing to know if its new-gnarled root
         Twists from York's head or belly of Lancaster;

         Or if a rational soul should stir, perchance,
765   Within the stem or summer shoot to advance
         Contrition's utmost throw, seeking in thee
         But oblivion, not thy forgiveness, FRANCE.

         as the young lizard extends his leopard spots
                 along the grass-blade seeking the green midge half an ant-size
770   and the Serpentine will look just the same
         and the gulls be as neat on the pond
         and the sunken garden unchanged
         and God knows what else is left of our London
                     my London, your London
775   and if her green elegance
                 remains on this side of my rain ditch
                 puss lizard will lunch on some other T-bone

         sunset grand couturier.

LXXXI

ZEUS lies in Ceres' bosom
    Taishan is attended of loves
        under Cythera, before sunrise
    and he said: " Hay aquí mucho catolicismo—(sounded
5   catoli*th*ismo)
        y muy poco reliHion "
and he said: " Yo creo que los reyes desaparecen "
(Kings will, I think, disappear)
That was Padre José Elizondo
10   in 1906 and in 1917
or about 1917
         and Dolores said: " Come pan, niño,"   eat bread, me lad
Sargent had painted her
            before he descended
15 (i.e. if he descended
        but in those days he did thumb sketches,
impressions of the Velázquez in the Museo del Prado
and books cost a peseta,
          brass candlesticks in proportion,
20 hot wind came from the marshes
    and death-chill from the mountains.
And later Bowers wrote: " but such hatred,
    I had never conceived such "
and the London reds wouldn't show up his friends
25   (i.e. friends of Franco
working in London) and in Alcázar
forty years gone, they said: go back to the station to eat
you can sleep here for a peseta "
        goat bells tinkled all night
30   and the hostess grinned: Eso es luto, *haw!*
mi marido es muerto
        (it is mourning, my husband is dead)

when she gave me paper to write on
with a black border half an inch or more deep,
35   say 5/8ths, of the locanda
" We call *all* foreigners frenchies "
and the egg broke in Cabranez' pocket,
            thus making history. Basil says
they beat drums for three days
40   till all the drumheads were busted
            (simple village fiesta)
and as for his life in the Canaries...
Possum observed that the local portagoose folk dance
was danced by the same dancers in divers localities
45   in political welcome...
the technique of demonstration
            Cole studied that (not G.D.H., Horace)
" You will find " said old André Spire,
that every man on that board (Crédit Agricole)
50   has a brother-in-law
                " You the one, I the few "
                said John Adams
speaking of fears in the abstract
        to his volatile friend Mr Jefferson.
55   (To break the pentameter, that was the first heave)
or as Jo Bard says: they never speak to each other,
if it is baker and concierge visibly
            it is La Rouchefoucauld and de Maintenon audibly.
" Te cavero le budella "
60   " La corata a te "
In less than a geological epoch
                said Henry Mencken
" Some cook, some do not cook
        some things cannot be altered"
65   Ἴυγξ. . . . . 'εμὸν ποτί δῶμα τὸν ἄνδρα
What counts is the cultural level,
        thank Benin for this table ex packing box

" doan yu tell nu one I made it "
                    from a mask fine as any in Frankfurt
70   " It'll get you offn th' groun "
                    Light as the branch of Kuanon
And at first disappointed with shoddy
the bare ram-shackle quais, but then saw the
high buggy wheels
75   and was reconciled,
George Santayana arriving in the port of Boston
and kept to the end of his life that faint *thethear*
of the Spaniard
                    as a grace quasi imperceptible
80   as did Muss the *v* for *u* of Romagna
and said the grief was a full act
                    repeated for each new condoleress
working up to a climax.
and George Horace said he wd/ " get Beveridge " (Senator)
85   Beveridge wouldn't talk and he wouldn't write for the **papers**
but George got him by campin' in his hotel
and assailin' him at lunch breakfast an' dinner
                    three articles
and my ole man went on hoein' corn
90   while George was a-tellin' him,
come across a vacant lot
                    where you'd occasionally see a wild rabbit
or mebbe only a loose one
                    AOI!
95   a leaf in the current
                                   at my grates no Althea

libretto   Yet
Ere the season died a-cold
Borne upon a zephyr's shoulder
100   I rose through the aureate sky
                    Lawes and Jenkyns guard thy rest
                    Dolmetsch ever be thy guest,

■ 97

Has he tempered the viol's wood
To enforce   both the grave   and the acute?
105 Has he curved us the bowl of the lute?
                    Lawes and Jenkyns guard thy rest
                    Dolmetsch ever be thy guest
Hast 'ou fashioned so airy a mood
        To draw up leaf from the root?
110 Hast 'ou found   a cloud   so light
        As seemed neither mist nor shade?

                    Then resolve me, tell me aright
                    If Waller sang or Dowland played.

                    Your eyen two wol sleye me sodenly
115   I may the beauté of hem nat susteyne

And for 180 years almost nothing.

Ed ascoltando al leggier mormorio
        there came new subtlety of eyes into my tent,
whether of spirit or hypostasis,
120   but what the blindfold hides
or at carneval
                            nor any pair showed anger
        Saw but the eyes and stance between the eyes,
colour, diastasis,
125   careless or unaware it had not the
        whole tent's room
nor was place for the full Εἰδώς
interpass, penetrate
        casting but shade beyond the other lights
130   sky's clear
            night's sea
            green of the mountain pool
            shone from the unmasked eyes in half-mask's space.
What thou lovest well remains,

135   the rest is dross
        What thou lov'st well shall not be reft from thee
        What thou lov'st well is thy true heritage
        Whose world, or mine or theirs
                                or is it of none?
140   First came the seen, then thus the palpable
                Elysium, though it were in the halls of hell,
        What thou lovest well is thy true heritage
        What thou lov'st well shall not be reft from thee

        The ant's a centaur in his dragon world.
145   Pull down thy vanity, it is not man
        Made courage, or made order, or made grace,
                Pull down thy vanity, I say pull down.
        Learn of the green world what can be thy place
        In scaled invention or true artistry,
150   Pull down thy vanity,
                                Paquin pull down!
        The green casque has outdone your elegance.

        " Master thyself, then others shall thee beare "
                Pull down thy vanity
155   Thou art a beaten dog beneath the hail,
        A swollen magpie in a fitful sun,
        Half black half white
        Nor knowst'ou wing from tail
        Pull down thy vanity
160   How mean thy hates
        Fostered in falsity,
                        Pull down thy vanity,
        Rathe to destroy, niggard in charity,
        Pull down thy vanity,
165   I say pull down.

        But to have done instead of not doing
                this is not vanity

To have, with decency, knocked
That a Blunt should open
170   To have gathered from the air a live tradition
or from a fine old eye the unconquered flame
This is not vanity.
        Here error is all in the not done,
all in the diffidence that faltered . . .

LXXXII

WHEN with his hunting dog I see a cloud
" Guten Morgen, Mein Herr " yells the black boy
from the jo-cart

(Jeffers, Lovell and Harley
5 also Mr Walls who has lent me a razor
  Persha, Nadasky and Harbell)

Swinburne my only miss
and I didn't know he'd been to see Landor
  and they told me this that an' tother
10 and when old Mathews went he saw the three teacups
  two for Watts Dunton who liked to let his tea cool,
So old Elkin had only one glory
  He did carry Algernon's suit case *once*
when he, Elkin, first came to London.
15 But given what I know now I'd have
  got thru it somehow...Dirce's shade
    or a blackjack.
When the french fishermen hauled him out he
recited 'em
20   might have been Aeschylus
  till they got into Le Portel, or wherever
in the original

    " On the Atreides' roof "
" like a dog...and a good job
25   ΕΜΟΣ ΠΟΣΙΣ...ΧΕΡΟΣ
    hac dextera mortus
    dead by this hand
believe Lytton first saw Blunt in the bull ring

as it might have been brother Packard

30 and " our brother Percy "

Basinio's manuscript with the

greek moulds in the margin

Otis, Soncino,

the " marble men " shall pass into nothingness,

35 Three birds on the wire

so requested Mr Clowes to sleep on the same

and as to who wd/ pay for the composition
if same were not used

(Elkin Mathews, my bantam)

40   After all " said Mr Birrell, " it is only the old story
of Tom Moore and Rogers "

Her Ladyship arose in the night

and moved all the furniture

(that is her Ladyship YX)

45 her Ladyship Z disliked dining alone and

The proud shall not lie by the proud

amid dim green lighted with candles

Mabel Beardsley's red head for a glory
Mr Masefield murmuring: Death

50   and Old Neptune meaning something unseizable

in a discussion of Flaubert

Miss Tomczyk, the medium
baffling the society for metaphysical research

and the idea that CONversation......

55   should not utterly wither
even I can remember

at 18 Woburn Buildings

Said Mr Tancred

of the Jerusalem and Sicily Tancreds, to Yeats,

60 " If you would read us one of your own choice

and

perfect

lyrics "

and more's the pity that Dickens died twice

65   with the disappearance of Tancred
   and for all that old Ford's conversation was better,
consisting in *res* non *verba,*
         despite William's anecdotes, in that Fordie
   never dented an idea for a phrase's sake

70   and had more humanitas jen

   (Cythera   Cythera)
With Dirce in one bark convey'd
Be glad poor beaste, love follows after thee
Till the cricket hops

75   but does not chirrp in the drill field
      8th day of September
         f   f
            d
               g
80   write the birds in their treble scale
Terreus!   Terreus!

      there are no righteous wars in " The Spring and Au-
                              tumn "
   that is, perfectly right on one side or the other

85   total right on either side of the battle line
         and the news is a long time moving
      a long time in arriving
            thru the impenetrable
crystalline, indestructible

90   ignorance of locality
The news was quicker in Troy's time
a match on Cnidos, a glow worm on Mitylene,
   Till forty years since, Reithmuller indignant:

" Fvy! in Tdaenmarck efen dh' beasantz gnow him,"
95   meaning Whitman, exotic, still suspect
        four miles from Camden
            " O troubled reflection
            " O Throat, O throbbing heart "
        How drawn, O GEA TERRA,
100   what draws as thou drawest
                till one sink into thee by an arm's width
        embracing thee. Drawest,
                truly thou drawest.
        Wisdom lies next thee,
105   simply, past metaphor.
    Where I lie let the thyme rise
                        and basilicum
            let the herbs rise in April abundant
    By Ferrara was buried naked, fu Nicolo
110   e di qua di la del Po,
    wind: 'ἐμὸν τὸν ἄνδρα
    lie into earth to the breast bone, to the left shoulder
            Kipling suspected it
        to the height of ten inches or over
115 man, earth : two halves of the tally
    but I will come out of this knowing no one
    neither they me
                connubium terrae   ἔφατα πόσις ἐμός
                                         ΧΘΟΝΙΟΣ, mysterium
120 fluid ΧΘΟΝΟΣ o'erflowed me
        lay in the fluid ΧΘΟΝΟΣ;
                that lie
    under the air's solidity
            drunk with ἸΧΩΡ of ΧΘΟΝΙΟΣ
125   fluid ΧΘΟΝΟΣ, strong as the undertow
            of the wave receding
    but that a man should live in that further terror, and live

the loneliness of death came upon me
    (at 3 P. M., for an instant)   δακρύων

130   ἐντεῦθεν

three solemn half notes
        their white downy chests black-rimmed
on the middle wire
       periplum

LXXXIII

ύδωρ
HUDOR et Pax
Gemisto stemmed all from Neptune
    hence the Rimini bas reliefs
5   Sd Mr Yeats (W. B.) " Nothing affects these people
        Except our conversation "
lux enim
    ignis est accidens   and,
wrote the prete in his edition of Scotus:
10   Hilaritas   the virtue *hilaritas*

the queen stitched King Carolus' shirts or whatever
while Erigena put greek tags in his excellent verses
    in fact an excellent poet, Paris
      toujours Pari'
15   (Charles le Chauve)

    and you might find a bit of enamel
    a bit of true blue enamel
      on a metal pyx or whatever
    omnia, quae sunt, lumina sunt, or whatever

20   so they dug up his bones in the time of De Montfort
      (Simon)

      Le Paradis n'est pas artificiel
and Uncle William dawdling around Notre Dame
in search of whatever
25   paused to admire the symbol
with Notre Dame standing inside it
Whereas in St Etienne

    or why not Dei Miracoli:
mermaids, that carving,

30   in the drenched tent there is quiet
      sered eyes are at rest

    the rain beat as with colour of feldspar
    blue as the flying fish off Zoagli
pax, ὕδωρ   ΎΔΩΡ
35   the sage
delighteth in water
    the humane man has amity with the hills

  as the grass grows by the weirs
     thought Uncle William *consiros*
40 as the grass on the roof of St What's his name
    near " Cane e Gatto "
     soll deine Liebe sein
  it would be about a-level the windows
     the grass would, or I dare say above that
45   when they bless the wax for the Palio

Olim de Malatestis
     with Maria's face there in the fresco
    painted two centuries sooner,
    at least that
50 before she wore it
    As Montino's
in that family group of about 1820
  not wholly Hardy's material

    or πάντα 'ρει

55 as he was standing below the altars
    of the spirits of rain

" When every hollow is full
            it moves forward "
      to the phantom mountain above the cloud
60   But in the caged panther's eyes:

                  " Nothing. Nothing that you can do..."

green pool, under green of the jungle,
caged: " Nothing, nothing that you can do."

Δρυάς, your eyes are like clouds

65   Nor can who has passed a month in the death cells
            believe in capital punishment
      No man who has passed a month in the death cells
            believes in cages for beasts

      Δρυάς, your eyes are like the clouds over Taishan
70   When some of the rain has fallen
            and half remains yet to fall

      The roots go down to the river's edge
            and the hidden city moves upward
            white ivory under the bark

75   With clouds over Taishan-Chocorua
            when the blackberry ripens
      and now the new moon faces Taishan
      one must count by the dawn star
            Dryad, thy peace is like water
80   There is September sun on the pools

      Plura diafana
            Heliads lift the mist from the young willows
      there is no base seen under Taishan

<pre>
              but the brightness of 'udor   ὕδωρ
85   the poplar tips float in brightness
        only the stockade posts stand

        And now the ants seem to stagger
                    as the dawn sun has trapped their shadows,
        this breath wholly covers the mountains
90   it shines and divides
        it nourishes by its rectitude
        does no injury
        overstanding the earth it fills the nine fields
                        to heaven

95   Boon companion to equity
              it joins with the process
                    lacking it, there is inanition

        When the equities are gathered together
        as birds alighting
100   it springeth up vital

        If deeds be not ensheaved and garnered in the heart
        there is inanition

              (have I perchance a debt to a man named Clower)

        that he eat of the barley corn
105   and move with the seed's breath

        the sun as a golden eye
                between dark cloud and the mountain

        " Non combaattere " said Giovanna
                    meaning, as before stated, don't work so hard
</pre>

110   don't

勿
助
長

        as it stands in the Kung-Sun Chow.
115   San Gregorio, San Trovaso
      Old Ziovan raced at seventy after his glories
              and came in long last
      and the family eyes stayed the same Adriatic
              for three generations (San Vio)
120   and was, I suppose, last month the Redentore as usual

      Will I ever see the Giudecca again?
            or the lights against it, Ca' Foscari, Ca' Giustinian
      or the Ca', as they say, of Desdemona
      or the two towers where are the cypress no more
125   or the boats moored off le Zattere
      or the north quai of the Sensaria   DAKRUŌN   ΔΑΚΡΥΩΝ

        and Brother Wasp is building a very neat house
        of four rooms, one shaped like a squat indian bottle
        La vespa, *la* vespa, mud, swallow system
130   so that dreaming of Bracelonde and of Perugia
      and the great fountain in the Piazza
      or of old Bulagaio's cat that with a well timed leap
         could turn the lever-shaped door handle
      It comes over me that Mr. Walls must be a ten-strike
135   with the signorinas
      and in the warmth after chill sunrise
      an infant, green as new grass,

has stuck its head or tip
out of Madame La Vespa's bottle

140   mint springs up again
                in spite of Jones' rodents
        as had the clover by the gorilla cage
                with a four-leaf

        When the mind swings by a grass-blade
145   an ant's forefoot shall save you
        the clover leaf smells and tastes as its flower

                The infant has descended,
                    from mud on the tent roof to Tellus,
        like to like colour he goes amid grass-blades
150   greeting them that dwell under XTHONOS   ΧΘΟΝΟΣ
        ΟΙ ΧΘΟΝΙΟΙ;   to carry our news
                    εἰς χθονίους   to them that dwell under the earth,
        begotten of air, that shall sing in the bower
                of Kore,   Περσεφόνεια
155   and have speech with Tiresias, Thebae

                Cristo Re, Dio Sole

        in about ½ a day she has made her adobe
        (la vespa) the tiny mud-flask

                and that day I wrote no further

160   There is fatigue deep as the grave.
        The Kakemono grows in flat land out of mist
                sun rises lop-sided over the mountain
                    so that I recalled the noise in the chimney
        as it were the wind in the chimney
165   but was in reality Uncle William

downstairs composing
that had made a great Peeeeacock
    in the proide ov his oiye
      had made a great peeeeeeecock in the...
170   made a great peacock
        in the proide of his oyyee

  proide ov his oy-ee
as indeed he had, and perdurable

a great peacock aere perennius
175   or as in the advice to the young man to
breed and get married (or not)
          as you choose to regard it

at Stone Cottage in Sussex by the waste moor
(or whatever) and the holly bush
180   who would not eat ham for dinner
because peasants eat ham for dinner
      despite the excellent quality
and the pleasure of having it hot

well those days are gone forever
185   and the traveling rug with the coon-skin tabs
and his hearing nearly all Wordsworth
      for the sake of his conscience but
preferring Ennemosor on Witches

did we ever get to the end of Doughty:
190   The Dawn in Britain?
                perhaps not
    Summons withdrawn, sir.)
  (bein' aliens in prohibited area)

```
        clouds lift their small mountains
195             before the elder hills

        A fat moon rises lop-sided over the mountain
        The eyes, this time my world,
                But pass and look from mine
                    between my lids
200                 sea, sky, and pool
                    alternate
                    pool, sky, sea,

        morning moon against sunrise
        like a bit of the best antient greek coinage


205             und

        Mir sagen
        Die Damen
        Du bist Greis,
                Anacreon


210     And that a Madonna novecento

        cd/ be as a Madonna quattrocento
        This I learned in the Tirol
                and as perfect
        where they paint the houses outside with figures
215     and the deep inner courts run back triple

                " Das heis' Walterplatz "
                heard in Bozen (Bolzano)
        and in my mother's time it was respectable,
        it was social, apparently,
220                     to sit in the Senate gallery
```

or even in that of the House
    to hear the fire-works of the senators
(and possibly representatives)
as was still done in Westminster in my time
225   and a very poor show from the once I saw it)

but if Senator Edwards cd/ speak
and have his tropes stay in the memory 40 years, 60 years?
in short / the descent
has not been of advantage either
230   to the Senate or to " society "
                      or to the people
    The States have passed thru a
           dam'd supercilious era
Down, Derry-down /
235   Oh let an old man rest.

LXXXIV

8th October:
        Si tuit li dolh elh plor
               Angold τέθνηκε
tuit lo pro, tuit lo bes
5   Angold τέθνηκε

" an' doan you think he chop an' change all the time
stubborn az a mule, sah, stubborn as a MULE,
got th' eastern idea about money "
              Thus Senator Bankhead

10 " am sure I don't know what a man like you
       would find to *do* here "
           said Senator Borah
Thus the solons, in Washington,
on the executive, and on the country, a.d. 1939

15 ye spotted lambe
       that is both blacke and white
is yeven to us for the eyes' delight

and now Richardson, Roy Richardson,
       says he is different
20 will I mention his name?

and Demattia is checking out.
      White, Fazzio, Bedell, *benedicti*
Sarnone, two Washingtons (dark) J and M
25   Bassier, Starcher, H. Crowder and
no soldier he although his name is Slaughter

this day October the whateverth   Mr. Coxey
aged 91 has mentioned bonds and their
                 interest

apparently as a basis of issue
30   and Mr Sinc Lewis has not
                  and Bartók has left us
        and Mr Beard in his admirable condensation
        (Mr Chas. Beard) has given one line to the currency
        at about page 426 " The Young Republic "
35   We will be about as popular as Mr John Adams
        and less widely perused
        and the he leopard lay on his back playing with straw
        in sheer boredom,
                  (Memoirs of the Roman zoo)
40   in sheer boredom
        Incense to Apollo
                  Carrara
                        snow on the marble
        snow-white
45   against stone-white
        on the mountain
        and as who passed the gorges between sheer cliffs
        as it might be by, is it the Garonne?
                  where one walks into Spagna
50   that T'ao Ch'ien heard the old Dynasty's music
            as it might be at the Peach-blossom Fountain
        where are smooth lawns with the clear stream
        between them, silver, dividing,

        and at Ho Ci'u destroyed the whole town
55   for hiding a woman, Κύθηρα δεινά
        and as Carson the desert rat said
        " when we came out we had
                  80 thousand dollars' worth "
                        (" of experience ")
60   that was from mining
                  having spent their capital on equipment
        but not cal'lated the time for return

and my old great aunt did likewise
with that too large hotel
65 but at least she saw damn all Europe
    and rode on that mule in Tangiers
        and in general had a run for her money

like Natalie
        " perhaps more than was in it "

70   Under white clouds, cielo di Pisa
out of all this beauty something must come,

O moon my pin-up,
            chronometer
Wei, Chi and Pi-kan
75 Yin had these three men full of humanitas (manhood)
            or jên²
Xaire Alessandro
            Xaire Fernando, e il Capo,
Pierre, Vidkun,
80   Henriot
and as to gradations
who went out of industrials into Government
    when the slump was in the offing
as against whom, prepense, got OUT of Imperial Chemicals
85 in 1938
so as not to be nourished by blood-bath?

quand vos venetz al som de l'escalina
                        ἦθος gradations
These are distinctions in clarity

90   ming² these are distinctions

John Adams, the Brothers Adam
there is our norm of spirit

our　中　chung[1]

whereto we may pay our
95   homage
Saith Micah:
                        Each in the name of...
So that looking at the sputtering tank of nicotine and
stale whiskey
100   (on its way out)
Kumrad Koba remarked:
                I will believe the American.
                                    Berlin 1945
the last appearance of Winston P.M. in that connection
105   e poi io dissi alla sorella
della pastorella dei suini:
e questi americani?
                si conducono bene?
ed ella: poco.
110   Poco, poco.
ed io: peggio dei tedeschi?
                ed ella: uguale, thru the barbed wire
                    you can, said Stef (Lincoln Steffens)
do nothing with revolutionaries
115   until they are at the end of their tether
and that Vandenberg has read Stalin, or Stalin, John Adams
is, at the mildest, unproven.

If the hoar frost grip thy tent
Thou wilt give thanks when night is spent.

NOTES

The first two systematic glosses of *The Pisan Cantos* were provided by John Hamilton Edwards' and William W. Vasse's *Annotated Index to the* Cantos *of Ezra Pound* (Berkeley: U. of Cal. Press, 1957) and by Achilles Fang's four-volume Harvard doctoral dissertation of 1958, "Materials for the Study of Pound's *Cantos.*" The '60s and '70s saw further exegetical work, much of which was published in *Paideuma: A Journal Devoted to Ezra Pound Scholarship*, founded in 1972 and edited by Carroll Terrell. The latter coordinated a team of eminent Pound scholars and synthesized several decades of research in his monumental two-volume *Companion to the* Cantos *of Ezra Pound* (U. of Cal. Press, 1980–84),—to which the reader is referred for more detailed annotation. While ineluctably (and most gratefully) indebted to Terrell's indispensible labors, the notes to the present edition take into account the additional scholarship devoted to *The Pisan Cantos* over the past twenty years, while also drawing on further commentaries provided by Peter Brooker, George Kearns, Christine Froula, William Cookson, Anthony Woodward, Mary de Rachewiltz, Massimo Bacigalupo, and Ronald Bush. The Greek in the text has been transliterated and the Chinese romanized (in the old Wade-Giles system) to facilitate pronunciation. Canto cross-references are given in bold type by Canto number followed by line number, thus: **78.36**. The text of these Cantos is that given in the 13th New Directions printing (1995), corrupt though it may be by purely philological standards. Richard Taylor's forthcoming variorum edition of *The Cantos* and Ronald Bush's study of the genesis and composition of the Pisans should clear up many questions.

CANTO 74

3. Third-century Persian founder of Manicheanism, flayed alive for his heretical teachings by the Zoroastrians. Rejecting all of the Old Testament and parts of the New, Mani (or Manes) claimed Buddha, Zoroaster, Hermes, and Plato as his predecessors and maintained he was the Paraclete promised by Christ.

4–6. After Benito Mussolini and his mistress Claretta Petacci were captured and summarily executed by partisans at Dongo, near Lake Como, on April 28, 1945, their bodies were brought to Milan and strung up by the heels in the Piazzale Loreto, thus "twice crucified." As a sacrificial victim, Mussolini (whose unofficial title, Il Duce, is often translated by Pound as "the Boss") evokes the symbolic slaying of Dionysus in the form of a bull (*bos* in Latin).

7. "Twice-born," Greek epithet for Dionysus, born once from his mother, Semele, and then from the thigh of his father, Zeus.

9–10. Pound's nickname for T.S. Eliot, whose poem "The Hollow Men" conceives the world as ending "Not with a bang but a whimper."

11. Deïoces, the first great ruler of the Medes, built the city of Ecbatana in the sixth century B.C.; according to Herodotus it was encircled by seven rising concentric walls in a variety of colors. "Dioce" has been heard by some commentators to rhyme with "Duce."

12. Canto 74 originally began here, before Pound changed its opening in November, appending the previous 11 lines which were typed on a separate sheet and perhaps at first withheld on account of their explicitly pro-Mussolinian tenor.

14. I.e. the Confucian Way or Truth (*tao*⁴).

14–18. Citations from the Confucian Classics, *The Unwobbling Pivot* I, 1, and *Mencius* III, 4, xiii, later translated by Pound: "After Confucius's death, when there was talk of regrouping, Tsang declined, saying: 'Washed in the Keang and Han, bleached in the autumn sun's-slope, what whiteness can one add to that whiteness, what candour?'"

19. Formed from the Latin *periplus*, a circumnavigation; defined in Canto 59 as "periplum, not as the land looks on a map/but as sea bord by men sailing." Here, the circuit of Helios, the sun.

20–21. The cliffs along the Strait of Gibraltar, traditionally known as the Pillars of Hercules, through which Dante's Ulysses passes before drowning near Mount Purgatory, where Lucifer fell to earth. Cf. *Inf.* XXVI and XXXIV. More or less due west of Gibraltar, North Carolina was the site of a (Luciferian?) meteor shower in 1944.

22. In Italian, a hot Mediterranean wind out of the southeast.

23. "OU TIS," Greek for "No Man" or "Nobody," the name Odysseus adopts to trick the Cyclops in Book IX of the *Odyssey*.

26. "Sister moon," i.e. Artemis/Diana?

28–31. Sigismundo Malatesta (1417–68), soldier and patron of the arts, constructed the Tempio Malatestiano in Rimini as a pagan monument to his love for his mistress (and later wife), Isotta degli Atti (?1430–70). The sculptor Agostino di Duccio (1418–81) was commissioned by him to supply its marble ornaments. Further examples of "precise definition": the paintings of Giovanni Bellini (?1430–1516) and the mosaics in the church of Santa Maria in the Trastevere district of Rome evoking "La Sposa" ("the bride") or "Sponsa Cristi" ("the bride of Christ").

33–46. Charlie Sung (or T.V. Soong), named premier of Chiang Kai-shek's China in June 1945 (as reported in *Time* magazine) and presumably bankrolled by anonymous ("anonimo") sources. As chancellor of the exchequer, Winston Churchill returned to the gold standard in 1925, thus depressing the value of the Indian currency to eighteen pence per hundred rupees. The primary tenet of Marxism was that workers should own the means of production, but Pound hoped to convert Stalin (whom he called "the best brain in politics today" in a May 8, 1945 interview) to his own economic views, which focused instead on the ownership of money or "the means of circulation."

48. A copy of the *Catholic Prayer Book for the Army and Navy / Pro Deo et Patria* was given to Pound by Father Aloysius H. Vath, the Roman Catholic chaplain of the DTC.

52. The original German title of Erich Maria Remarque's antiwar novel, *All Quiet on the Western Front* (1929).

55. For the paradisal properties of sapphire, see Dante, *Pur.* I, 13.

56–59. A paraphrase of *Mencius* IV, ii, 11, with an etymological reading of the characters mentioned in Legge's note.

60–61. W.H.D. Rouse (1863–1950), classical scholar and translator of the *Odyssey*, discovered in his travels through the Aegean that tales similar to those surrounding Odysseus were still being told about Elias (or Elijah), the Hebrew prophet who tells of the coming of the redeemer.

64–75. In native Australian mythology, the god Wondjina (his name here rhymed with the Chinese "Ouan Jin" [or *wen*²-*jen*²], meaning "Man of Letters") brought the world into being by saying the names of things; fearing he had thereby created too many objects, his father had his mouth removed. Douglas Fox, a student of the German archaeologist Leo Frobenius (1873–1938) and who was in correspondence with Pound about his research among the Australian aborigines in the '30s, provided the following commentary on the legend: "As one old man explained, if Ungar [the father] had not very wisely done as he did, then the blackfellow would have been burdened with all the glittering claptrap of the white man's culture and would not have been able to devote himself properly to the important things of life: conversation, dancing, hunting and warfare."

75–76. "In the beginning was the Word/the Holy Ghost or the perfect Word: sincerity." Cf. John 1.1, included in the *Catholic Prayer Book* as "The Last Gospel." Cf. also the "Prayers to the Holy Spirit": "We beseech Thee, O Lord, that the Paraclete Who proceedeth from Thee may enlighten our minds and lead us, as Thy son hath promised, into all truth."

77–85. T'ai Shan, or Great Mountain, a sacred site in China's Shantung province, here visually rhymed with one of the mountains in the Apuan Alps to the northeast of the DTC—just as Fujiyama, the sacred mountain of Japan, is glimpsed in the Alpine scenery of the northern Italian Lake Garda, site of the villa where the Roman poet Catullus wrote his salutation to the promontory of Sirmio, the movement of whose waters evokes the onomatopoetic epithet "poluphloisboios" (or "loud-roarings") attributed by Homer to the sea.

86–91. Gioacchino Nicoletti, prefect of the town of Gardone Riviera, not far from Salò, provisional capital of the puppet Social Republic which Mussolini established in late September 1943 after having been dismissed by King Victor Emmanuel and replaced by Marshal Badoglio, who negotiated an armistice with the Allies. Pound visited Lake Garda in November 1943 in order to make contact with elements of the Salò regime. Translation: "The Woman... the woman... the woman!" [perhaps Clara Petacci, who had followed Mussolini to Salò], "Why must it go on?" "If I fall... I shall not fall on my knees," a defiant statement attributed to Bianca Capello (?1547–87), mistress of Francesco de' Medici, Duke of Tuscany.

93. The African legend of Gassire's Lute is recorded in Leo Frobenius' *African Genesis* (1937); cf. **198** below. The legend includes the apostrophe, "Hooh! Fasa!" or "Hail to the tribe of Fasa" (echoing the Italian *fascio*?).

96–97. "Under six gallows... Absolve, may you absolve us all." From the "Ballade des Pendus" of François Villon (1431-?65), whose poem *Le Testament* provides one of the models for *The Pisan Cantos.*

97–100. Barabbas, Christ's companion in captivity, here associated with two of Pound's companions in Paris in the 1920s, the writer Ernest Hemingway (1898–1961) and the composer George Antheil (1900–59), and with his fellow prisoners at the DTC, whose names follow.

105. Lesbia plays teasingly with her sparrow in Catullus 2.

107–10. "And the sad thought returns/toward Ussel. To Ventadour/goes desire, retrieving time." Pound's medievalizing Italian may echo *Pur.* VIII, 1–6.

109–19. Pound traveled through the troubadour country of southern France in the summers of 1912, 1919, and 1924, visiting, among other places, the towns of Ussel, Ventadour, Limoges, and Excideuil (where Mme Pujol kept an inn). Urochs are represented in the paleolithic cave paintings of Font de Gaumes, near Les Eyzies.

129. Marble from the nearby quarry of Carrara was used in the construction of the leaning tower of Pisa.

131. Japanese form of Kuan-yin, the Chinese goddess of mercy.

132–35. Bishops of Rome in the first century, among the list of Apostles and Martyrs invoked in the *Catholic Prayer Book*. The design on the back of the priest's chasuble at a mass held at the DTC may have suggested the image of the scarab at the altar.

137–38. Ideogram: *hsien³*, "manifest, display, be illustrious." Contains the radicals for sun and moon and silk and is sometimes translated by Pound as "tensile light descending."

138. "Virtue," glossed by Pound in his Confucian translations as "The *virtù*, i.e. this self-knowledge [looking straight into the heart and acting hence] is the root."

139. "Are lights." From the Latin of the medieval Neoplatonic philosopher (and heretic) John Scotus Erigena (?810–?77): "Omnia, quae sunt, lumina sunt." Cf. 155–57 below: "all things that are are lights."

140–45. Shun, Yao, Yu, three legendary early rulers of China, often referred to in the Confucian classics as paragons of virtuous statecraft.

146. Large guard towers at the four corners of the DTC stockade.

150–52. Cf. Isaiah 1:27: "Zion shall be redeemed by justice, and those in her who repent, by righteousness." As opposed, presumably, to the policies of "David rex," i.e. King David ("the prime s.o.b." omitted from the 1949 Faber edition).

155. The "Oirishman " is Scotus Erigena and "King Carolus," the Holy Roman Emperor Charles II, grandson of Charlemagne.

158–60. The body of Erigena was supposedly ("soi disantly") exhumed as part of a witch hunt against Manichean heretics—although there is no record of this (it was the bones of his disciple, Amaury de Bène, that were dug up and scattered in 1210). "Les Albigeois," or Albigensians, were persecuted and eventually destroyed in a crusade against heresy launched by Simon de Montfort in the 13th century.

161–69. Themistocles won the battle of Salamis in ships built by money loaned by the state of Athens and not by private banks—an early example of Social Credit. The Soviet statesman Lenin is quoted ("dixit Lenin") attacking the war-profiteering of the international arms industry.

163. "A time to speak, a time to be silent" (Eccl: 3:7), Malatesta's motto, inscribed on Isotta's tomb in the Tempio.

170. Pound observed the Italian Fascist calendar, in which all events were dated from Mussolini's March on Rome in 1922. 1945 was thus year 23.

171–73. Louis Till, an African-American trainee at the DTC executed on July 2, 1945, here mythologically associated with Zeus's ram, whose golden fleece Jason and the Argonauts hunted in the kingdom of Colchis. Till was the father of Emmet Till, whose cold-blooded murder at age fourteen by two white men in Mississippi in 1955 sparked the Civil Rights Movement in the South.

176–77. Ideogram: *mo⁴*, " not, no," echoing the Greek "No man" and visually evoking "a man on whom the sun has gone down."

180. In the Noh play, *Hagoromo* (translated by Pound in 1916), the word refers to the "feather-mantle" left hanging by an "aerial spirit" (or *tennin*) on a bough, where it is discovered by a priest; in order to retrieve her magical cloak, the nymph agrees to teach him a dance symbolic of the daily changes of the moon.

184. Russian for "comrade" (referring to another trainee or to Pound himself?).

190–91. "Either Cythera [i.e. Aphrodite] or Ixotta [cf. 28 above] or in St. Mary of the

Miracles." This Venetian church contains sculptures of sirens by Pietro Lombardo (1435–1515), much admired by Pound.

196. A quote from *Mencius* IV, 8, iv.

198. "Of Italy betrayed" (when Mussolini was replaced as head of the government by Marshal Badoglio in July 1943).

197–202. The Soninke legend "Gassire's Lute" recorded by Frobenius (cf. **93** above) tells of the four destructions (by vanity, falsehood, greed, and dissension) and four rebuildings of the mythical four-gated female city of Wagadu, a city "not of stone, not of wood, not of earth," but embodying "the strength which lives in the hearts of men and in the wombs of women." Its eventual fifth reconstruction in the future rhymes with Pound's eschatological dream of "city of Dioce" (cf. **11** above): "Should Wagadu ever be found for the fifth time, then she will live so forcefully that vanity, falsehood, greed and dissension will never be able to harm her."

204. Greek goddess of fertility.

206. "In counterpoint."

208–9. "That softens[Dante, *Pur.* VIII, 2]/to the left of the Tower [of Pisa]."

211. "Who forgets and lets himself fall," from the Provençal of troubadour Bernart de Ventadorn's "Lark Song."

212–13. Book XI of the *Odyssey* recounts Odysseus's descent (or *nekuia*) into Hades, where he sees the shades of Alcmene and Tyro. In Book XII, he must navigate his way between the whirlpool of Charybdis and the sharp rocks of Scylla.

219. I.e. hamadryad, or tree nymph.

220. I.e. "vae soli," from Eccl. 4:10 ("woe to him who is alone"), via Pound's translation of Jules Laforgue's "Pierrots: Scène court mais typique."

224. "HELION PERI HELION" ("The sun around the sun").

226. Epithet of Diana, the moon-goddess; also the name of the Roman goddess of childbirth.

230–35. Basil Bunting (1900–85), jailed as conscientious objector in 1918, conducted a hunger strike in prison. His collection of poems, *Redimiculum Matellarum* ("A Garland of Chamberpots"), was published in 1930.

240. Joe Gould (1889–1957), Greenwich Village bohemian, author of the apocryphal *Oral History of Our Times*. Edward Estlin Cummings (1894–1962), imprisoned by the French army at the end of WWI, as recounted in *The Enormous Room* (1922).

245. "It is finished, Go," Latin formula used at the end of mass, derived from Christ's final words on the cross.

247–63. Memories of Pound's 1908 stay in Gibraltar: Raisuli (1875–1925), a Moroccan brigand, kidnapped Ion Perdicaris in 1904 and held him for ransom, causing an international incident; Elson, a missionary with whom Pound stayed in Gibraltar.

265. "Color of light."

267. From Pound's 1911 translation of the Anglo-Saxon poem *The Seafarer*: "Grey-haired he groaneth, knows gone companions,/Lordly men are to earth o'ergiven."

269–76. An enumeration of shades: Ford Madox [Hueffer] Ford (1873–1939), English novelist, poet, and editor; William Butler Yeats (1865–1939), Irish poet; James Joyce (1882–1939), Irish novelist; Victor Plarr (1863–1929), British poet; Edgar Jepson (1863–1938), English novelist; Maurice Hewlett (1861–1923), English novelist and poet; Sir Henry Newbolt (1862–1938), English poet.

280. Colonel Goleyevsky, White Russian émigré and former tsarist military attaché, a friend of the Pounds in Paris in the '20s.

286–92. Restaurants remembered: Paris (Bouiller, Closerie des Lilas, Voisin's), London (Dieudonné), St. Petersburg (the cake shops on the Nevsky Prospekt), Vienna (Schöner's), Bolzano (Der Greif), New York (Mouquin's, Robert's).

288. George Holden Tinkham (1870–1956), isolationist congressman from Massachusetts whom Pound met in Venice in 1936. REI PANTA, "all things flow" (Heraclitus).

296. William Henry Hudson (1841–1922), naturalist and novelist.

297. Misprint for "Où sont les heures" ("Where are the joys,"), a variation on Villon's "Où sont les neiges d'antan" ("Where are the snows of yesteryear").

298. Henry James (1843–1916), the American novelist, and his housekeeper at Rye, England, Mrs. Hawkesby.

301–4. Henry Brooks Adams (1838–1918); the "monument" who relayed the anecdote was the Harvard-educated philosopher and Rome resident, George Santayana (1863–1952).

305. I.e. "Haec sunt fasti" ("Here then are the festivals listed in the calendar").

306. Bastille Day (July 14), 1945.

307–14. *Time* magazine of June 25, 1945: an obituary for the popular novelist Amélie Rives (1864–1945), whom Pound knew from London and later in Rome during his broadcasting days; a photo resembling the equestrian portrait of Scottish traveler Cunninghame Grahame (1852–1936); the German chemical factory I.G. Farben still intact, to the strains of the signature WWII song, "Lillibullero"—whereas the architecture of the old hotel Adelphi on London's Strand has been destroyed by remodeling (?).

317–20. Henry Hudson Edwards, the G.I. who made a writing table for Pound out of a packing box; his African-American features are associated with the Baluba (i.e. Biembe) masks from the Congo studied by Frobenius.

328. "Nothing else."

331–33. "Ye shall do no unrighteousness in judgment, in meteyard, in weight, or in measure" (Lev. 19:35). "And that ye study to be quiet, and to do your business, and to work with your own hands, as we commanded you" (1Thess. 4:11).

340. "For all people will walk every one in the name of his god" (Micah 4:5)—Pound extracting a tolerant polytheism ("temples/plural") from the Old Testament.

341–45. Terracina, site on Italy's western seacoast associated with the birth of Venus and, Pound dreamt, locus of a future shrine reestablished in her honor. Virgil's *Aeneid* (I, 404) records that Anchises, father of Aeneas, recognized Aphrodite from her gait when she approached him in human guise.

348. A cluster of stars said to be composed of the seven daughters of Atlas.

352. "Chthonia gea, Mêter" ("nether earth, Mother").

359. "TITHONOI." The goddess Eos transformed Tithonos into a grasshopper (or katydid) so that she might hear her lover's song forever.

361. "In coitus illumination."

362–70. Aphrodite-like Olga Rudge, henna-haired, dressed in the latest fashions of Drecol or Lanvin, like a figure out of Manet's painting of the bar at the Folies Bergère—the painterly tradition of 19th-century France ("la France dixneuvième"), represented by Edouard Manet (1832–83), Edgar Degas (1834–1917), and Constantin Guys (1802–92), continuing on into the Fauviste work of Maurice Vlaminck (1876–1905), according to his friend the French poet and critic writer Fritz Vanderpyl (1876–1950).

372. "It would rest without further tossing" (*Inf.* XXVII, 63).

373–74. When seized by the partisans at his house at Sant'Ambrogio above Rapallo (overlooking the Tyrrhenian Sea), Pound picked up along the hill path a eucalyptus pip which he kept with him at Pisa as a talismanic mnemonic device.

375–77. Memories of Parisian restaurants leading to memories of his walking tours in southern France (cf. **107ff.**).

379–81. "The beautiful Tower" (of Pisa), associated with the so-called Tower of Hunger, also in Pisa, where Ugolino della Gheradesca (?1212–89), accused of treason, was imprisoned with his sons and grandsons. Dante (*Inf.* XXXII–XXXIII) pictures him starving to death.

382. Presumably to elude the military censor, Pound refers to Hitler and Mussolini only by their initial letters.

384–85. "Frobenius the privy councilor/who created thunder in Baluba." While exploring a remote region of the Congo in 1905, Frobenius' party came under attack; they were saved, however, when an enormous thunderstorm erupted. The local Baluba (i.e. Biembe) tribesmen therefore referred to him in their drum language as the "white rainmaker."

386–87. Jean Cocteau (1891–1963), French poet and playwright; T.S. Eliot (see **9**).

388. "Poor and old never did I read a letter" (from Villon's "Ballade Pour Prier Nostre Dame")

390. From Villon's "Paradis peint où sont harpes et luths" ("Painted paradise where are harps and lutes") in "Ballade Pour Prier Nostre Dame."

393. "Great NIGHT of the soul."

395. "Companion[s] of misery," referring to Pound's fellow prisoners, here named.

401. Dukes Mixture, the name of the tobacco ration alloted to the trainees, bags of which served as the unit of exchange in commercial transactions among the prisoners.

403. "And I too in the pigsty," referring to Circe's transformation of Odysseus' crew into swine in Book X of the *Odyssey*.

405. "I went into the pigsty and saw the corpses of souls"

410. Carrol Crawford, a fellow prisoner, named after the revolutionary leader Charles Carroll of Carrollton (1737–1832), just as many other African-American trainees in the DTC bore the names of early American presidents.

411. "THELGEIN" ("to enchant, betwitch, cheat").

414. "Nor fair-tressed Circe, well!," "kaka phurgak' edôken" ("she had given them evil drugs"—*Od.* X, 213).

416. Misprint for "veleno" ("poison").

419. The son of a blacksmith, Mussolini was born at Predappio, in Romagna.

419–25. Allen Upward (1863–1926), cultural anthropologist and world traveler, wrote in a 1915 poem, "I withstood the savages of the Niger with a revolver:/I withstood the savages of the Thames with a printing press." The cover of his comparative study of religions, *The Divine Mystery* (1910), featured the seal of Sitalkas ("Prohibitor of Corn-Growing'); he committed suicide in the end. "Until I end my song"—cf. Eliot's *The Waste Land*, "Sweet Thames, run softly, till I end my song" (from Spenser's "Prothalamion").

427. Matteo da Pasti (d. 1448) and Antonio Pisano (?1397–1455) both made intaglio medallions of Sigismundo Malatesta and his circle.

435–44. Snippets from the Confucian *Analects* .

445–46. "And at the crossing of the three roads, Cunizza/and the other woman: 'I am the Moon.'" Reminiscence of a visionary encounter recorded in the drafts of the Italian Cantos 74–75 composed by Pound in January-February 1945 and later abandoned. In these drafts, standing at the *triedro* ("trihedron') or symbolic crossing of three paths near Sant'Ambrogio (in turn evocative of "Trivia," the Latin epithet of Diana as goddess of crossroads), Basinio Basini (1425–57), the court poet of Sigismundo Malatesta and *persona* of Pound, sees the apparition of Cunizza da Romano (1198–1279), lover of the troubadour poet Sordello and, because she freed her brother's slaves, symbol of Kuanon-like compassion. Dante places Cunizza in the Third Heaven of Love (see Cantos 6 and 29).

449–50. "Night of the soul," here associated with the wisdom addressed to posterity ("ad posteros") by the Spanish mystic St. John of the Cross (1542–91).

455. "The old woman in [Voltaire's] *Candide*" who, in a parody of the *Odyssey*, undergoes a series of Job-like misfortunes in the course of her travels.

457. "Paradise is not artificial," cf. Charles Baudelaire's study of drugs, *Les Paradis artificiels* (1860).

458. "Splintered."

462. Lake Nemi, site of the sacred grove and temple of Diana, guarded by a priest who held the post until killed by another who sought the office. Cf. Frazer, *The Golden Bough* (1890).

466. Either Nietzsche's Dionysian hero Zarathustra or Zoroaster, the religious teacher of ancient Persia. Both are obsolete ("desuet"), unless this also refers to Lake Nemi.

467. The "small castle," a hill near Pound's house in Sant'Ambrogio.

471–75. "Immemorial of Athena/glaux, glaukôpis" ("little owl, with glinting eyes/olive trees"). Pound was quite struck by the explanation given by Allen Upward (cf. **419** above) of the Homeric epithet *glaukôpis* ascribed to Athena: "The property of the *glaux* [owl] and olive leaf, to shine and then not to shine, 'glint' rather than shine. Certainly a more living word if one lives among olive yards."

476. "North Wind, East Wind, South Wind."

477. "There's the bogeyman."

479–80. "The Little Well/at Tigullio," beach at Rapallo.

483. "The descendants of Remus the magnanimous."

489–90. Cf. Pound's translation of the *Analects* VII, XIII: "In Ch'i he [Confucius] heard the 'Shao' (cf. **519** below) sung, and for three months did not know the taste of meat; said: didn't figure the performance of music had attained to that summit."

491–92. "Ligur," alludes to the "clear, shrill" song of the sirens in Homer. Pound glimpsed the combined processes of the sun and the legendary emperor Shun's song (cf. **520** below) in the components of the Chinese ideogram *shao*.

493. Japanese verse form of five lines.

495. In Pound's first Canto, Elpenor, the ill-fated member of Odysseus' crew who died falling off the roof of Circe's house, asks that he be remembered by the epitaph: "A man of no fortune and with a name to come."

496–97. President John Adams' fulminations against banks of discount struck a sympathetic chord in Pound—the most recent example of their financial machinations being the revaluation of gold from $21.65 to $35 an oz. during the Roosevelt administration.

500–8. Jewish financiers: Meyer Amschel Rothschild (1743–1812), founder of the House of Rothschild, Henry Morgenthau, Sr. (1856–1946), banker and real estate magnate, Henry Morgenthau, Jr. (1891–1967), Roosevelt's Secretary of the Treasury, Israel Moses Sieff (1889–1972), English banker and reputed anonymous owner of the London *Daily Mirror*.

507. Cf. H. Gordon Selfridge, *The Romance of Commerce* (1923).

514. "oversalted, spoiled."

515–16. Cf. 150: "to redeem Zion with justice."

517–31. Foundational moments of Chinese history (the *shao* or succession dances marking the peaceful accessions of the legendary emperors Shun and Y'u to the throne), here juxtaposed with the Old Testament, apparently in an attempt to reveal the foundations of Judaic law (betrayed by modern-day Jewish financiers?) in Leviticus 19:35 (cf. 331 above). Jeremiah 31:38–39 contains instructions for the rebuilding of Jerusalem after a new covernant has been established with the Lord ("the city shall be built to the Lord from the tower of Hananeel unto the gate of the corner"). In Jeremiah 32:8–9, the prophet, shut up "in the court of the prison" in Babylon-occupied Jerusalem, is inspired by the Lord to purchase a field "in Anathoth, which is in the country of Benjamin" for seventeen shekels of silver, a first step toward the reestablishment of the destroyed kingdom of Judah.

528. Mount Chocorua in eastern New Hampshire, Olga Rudge's childhood summer home.

539–40. "If those who use a currency give it up in favor of another," from Aristotle's *Politics*, 1275b, 16.

546. Deleted in the 1949 Faber edition.

552–67. Pound was a proponent of the stamp scrip introduced in the Austrian town of Wörgl, which he visited in 1935. Called *Schwundgeld* or "disappearing money," this locally issued currency lost its value if not spent within a certain period of time—an incentive against the hoarding of money, designed to increase the circulation of goods and services.

570. The N.E.P. or New Economic Plan, launched by Lenin (in 1921) to reinvigorate the Soviet economy; it did not, however, include the Poundian nostrum of the work-certificate (credit extended to workers for work done) and was thus doomed to failure.

577. Cf. 340.

578–83. Aristotle, *Nicomachean Ethics*, 1095a.

585–92. Confucian ethics, as embodied by China's legendary emperors. From *The Unwobbling Pivot* VI.

593–94. When asked what he would have done had his father been guilty of murder, Emperor Shun replied that he would have taken his father ("son père") on his back and retired into anonymity on the seacoast—an example of Confucian filial piety.

597. "Hail to Great Japan."

598–600. The title characters of two Noh plays translated by Pound in 1916, the former an old blind man vainly sought after by his daughter, the latter a ghost returning to praise his slayer.

601. "Because it is impossible." From the Church Father Tertullian's insistence on faith over reason.

605. "KORE, AGLAOS ALAOU" ("Daughter [i.e. Persephone], the radiance of the blind one [i.e. Tiresias?].

606–9. Baron Wester Wemyss (1864–1933), monocled admiral of the fleet and signer of the WWI armistice on behalf of the Allies, here all wet.

610. Silvio Gesell (1862–1930), finance minister of the first (independent socialist) Munich Councils Republik in 1919, of which the anarchist Gustav Landauer (1870–1919) was the education minister before being arrested and assassinated by the Social Democratic authorities. Pound was a student of Gesell's radical monetary theories.

614. "The money is there," a statement made to Mussolini in 1943 by Gianpetro Pellegrini of the Salò Republic's Ministry of Finance when offering him a handsome monthly sum for his personal expenses (initially declined).

619. Persephone, goddess of the Underworld.

620. "That leans."

621. Pontius Pilate, Roman procurator of Judaea (c. 26–37).

625–26. Alfred von Tirpetz (1849–1930), German admiral who developed U-boat warfare against the allies in WWI, warning his daughter against the sirenlike ("SEIRENES") charms of high-ranking naval officers.

626. The solar swastika of Hindu tradition?

630. "In lieu of."

633. "CHARITES," in Homer, The Graces.

637. "To the coast."

639. "A white-colored shell" (cf. Botticelli's painting *The Birth of Venus*).

642–43. "The southwest wind blows." The Noh play *Suma Genji*, translated by Pound in 1916, climaxes with the "supernatural apparition" of its hero Genji ("a sort of place-spirit") on the seashore of Suma—here rhymed with the theophany of Venus.

645. Cf. 212.

646. "Europe and unchaste Pasiphaë." Europa was raped by Zeus in the form of a bull; Pasiphaë, wife of King Minos, was the mother of the Minotaur.

647. The Southeast and East Winds.

648. Cf. 445–46.

650. "The Tarpeian Cliff," a place in Rome where criminals and traitors were hurled to their death. At **76.45**, it is a Roman restaurant.

651. Common Roman wine.

652–53. Cf. 577. "Come spirit/come."

654. Aristotle, native of Stagira.

655–56. The West and East Winds.

658. "Brododactylos," Aeolic form (via Sappho) of Homer's "rosy-fingered" dawn.

661. "Against the light." Evokes a photograph of Olga Rudge.

662. Cf. "Pisanello lacking the skill/To forge Achaia" [i.e. to recreate Greece] in Pound's 1920 poem "Mauberley."

664. "Venus, Cythera, or Rhodes" (cf. Horace, *Odes* I.vii.1)

665. "Ligurian wind, come."

666–75. Aubrey Beardsley (1872–98), English illustrator, associated with the Symbolists and Decadents; John Kettlewell, a student at Oxford in 1913, when Edward, Prince of Wales ("Edvardus") began his studies there; William Lawrence (1889–1915), younger brother of T.E. Lawrence (1888–1935), invited Pound to speak on Cavalcanti at Oxford in 1913. Lines 667–74 were deleted in the 1949 Faber edition.

676. A German-initiated project to build a railroad linking western Europe to the Persian Gulf, 1888–1904.

677–80. Pound may have been shown T.E. Lawrence's recent photos of the ancient cliff city Arabia Petraea by his brother William. T.E. Lawrence attended the 1919 Versailles Peace Conference with the Arab delegation, but was disgusted with the power politics played by the English prime minister, Lloyd George ("L.L.G"), and its French convener, Georges Clemenceau ("the frogbassador").

685–91. Thomas Collins, lecturer in English at Oxford, took part in the discussion after Pound read his paper on Cavalcanti there in 1913, quoting a line of Sappho ("*phanatei moi*," or "he seems to me") to prove her superiority to Cavalcanti's line "causing the air to tremble." Magdalen, a college of Oxford University. "The Hound of Heaven," a celebrated poem by Francis Thompson (1859–1907), published in 1893.

704. "Battling" Siki, Senegalese in origin, heavyweight boxing champion of the 1920s.

711–12. "That guy Stalin," whose boyhood nickname was Koba, or "the bear."

713. Ernest Rhys (1859–1946), English editor.

717. I.e. "buggered."

720. The muses of history and dance, respectively.

721. Probably Harley Granville-Barker (1877–1946), English actor and playwright.

724. "Essomenoisi," cf. *Od.* XI, 76, "for generations to come."

725. "The grove wants an altar."

726. Lucrezia Borgia (1480–1519).

727–30. "A pleasant quarter-hour (in the Malestiana Library)." Located in the town of Cesena, the library was directed by Manlio Torquato Dazzi, who assisted Pound during the early '20s in his research into the life and times of Sigismundo Malatesta.

730–33. Quotes from earlier Cantos dealing with historical themes.

734–37. G.R.S. Mead (1863–1933), editor of a quarterly review devoted to occult subjects such as reincarnation. The Fortean Society was similarly dedicated to the investigation of unusual and unexplained natural phenomena.

744. "The Birth" (of Venus), by Botticelli.

745–47. The Palazzo Capoquardi Salimbene, Olga Rudge's residence in Siena during the '30s, contains a panel painting with a child's face which reminded Pound of their daughter, Mary.

749. From Pound's 1945 Italian translation of *L'Asse che non vacilla*. His 1947 English version (*The Unwobbling Pivot* X) runs: "The *unmixed* functions [in time and space] without bourne." Cf. **80.673.**

752. "In a prepared place," from Calvacanti's "Donna mi prega," also translated by Pound as "in a sacred place" or "the formèd trace."

753. "Spider brings me good luck."

754. "EIKONES," pictures, images, icons.

755–56. Cf. **30** above.

759–81. Early memories of New York City: "black Jim," a servant at the boarding house on 47th Street run by the Weston branch of Pound's family, later replaced by the Ritz-Carlton. Among its residents in the 1890s: the architect John Fouquet, the real estate agent John Quackenbush, known for his goatee ("barbiche"), the musician Kate Chittenden. Other New York sights and sounds: Mouquin's, the French restaurant; former presidential candidate George Francis Train, now an urban vagrant; the various baubles Pound's Aunt Frank had brought back from her European voyages.

782. One of Pound's ancestors, Joseph Wadsworth, stole the Connecticut charter and hid it in the Charter Oak.

783–88. Various stops along Pound's and Aunt Frank's 1898 and 1902 grand tours of

Europe, the visits to the Al Hambra in Granada and "the gallery of Queen Lindaraja" leading to Gibraltar and Tangiers. Cf. **247–63** above.

789–90. James Joyce located Calypso's island near Gibraltar and the Pillars of Hercules. His novel *Ulysses* ends with Molly Bloom's memories of her girlhood in Gibraltar.

794–803. "See Naples [and die]," Italian proverb in praise of the city's beauty, here contrasted with the loveliness of northern Italy: the romanesque Church of San Michele in Pavia, the romanesque church of San Zeno Maggiore in Verona (which contains the column signed "Adamo made me"), the frescoes in Verona's San Pietro Martire, Stefano da Verona's painting *Madonna in the Garden*, and the "Restaurant of the (twelve) Apostles" in Verona, where the headwaiter pointed out "Here is the tea" to the young busboy (the "piccolo").

799–800. "And 'make the air tremble with clarity,'" a signature line of Cavalcanti's, as given in one of the manuscripts Pound consulted at the Capitolare Library in Verona for his 1932 edition of Cavalcanti's *Rime*.

809–12. George Washington Carver (?1864–1943), African-American discoverer of many new uses for peanuts ("arachidi"). During the war, Pound tried to persuade a number of bureaucrats in Italy that the cultivation of peanuts would solve Italy's food shortages—just as he later had syrup-producing American maples planted near Brunnenburg Castle in the South Tyrol, but in the process only managed to introduce poison ivy into the region.

819–25. Pound's daughter, Mary, was raised in the Italian Tyrol; through her he met the Bacher family, whose wood carvings blended folk art with an intaglio technique worthy of Pisanello's medals of Malatesta.

828. Lines refracting the poems "Clair de Lune" and "Fountain Court (à Arthur Symons)" by the Symbolist Paul Verlaine (1844–96).

836–38. "And is not an attribute. . . it is an agent." Medieval scholastic distinctions found in commentaries on Cavalcanti's "Donna mi prega," a philosophical canzone that investigates the relation of memory to desire. Pound's full translation of Cavalcanti's poem provides the centerpiece of Canto 36 and its "light philosophy" suffuses the entire Pisan sequence.

839. Pound observes in his essay on Cavalcanti that the rose form made by the magnet in iron filings is a perfect example of energy realizing itself as pattern.

839–40. Cf. Ben Jonson's "Her Triumph" (in his 1624 *Celebration of Charis*): "Ha' you felt the wool of beaver/Or swan's down ever?/Or have smelt o' the bud o' the briar?/Or the nard in the fire?" John Dowland's setting of this poem was published by Arnold Dolmetsch (cf. **81.**100–13).

842. The river of forgetfulness in Hades. In Dante's sacred geography, however, the stream is placed on the summit of Mount Purgatory. Cf. *Pur.* XXVIII, 127–31: "On this side it descends with virtue that takes from one the memory of sin; on the other side it restores the memory of every good deed. Here Lethe, so on the other side Eunoe it is called; and it works not if first it be not tasted on this side and on that" (Singleton). In the autograph draft of Canto 74, the final lines originally read: "We who have passed over Lethe/seeking Eunoe." Under the guidance of Matelda, Dante drinks of the waters of Lethe in *Pur.* XXXI and of Eunoe (from the Greek, "well-minded") in *Pur.* XXXIII.

CANTO 75

3. Gerhart Münch (1907–88), pianist, composer, and arranger, native of Dresden, Germany, recently fire-bombed by the Allies (hence the allusion to Phlegethon, the flaming river of fire in Hades?). Münch provided an "abbreviation" for the violin of Francesco da Milano's sixteenth-century version of "Le Chant des Oiseaux" by the French composer Clément Jannequin (?1485–1558), whose score (in Olga Rudge's hand) is given below.

5–6. Dietrich Buxtehude (1637–1707), German composer; Ludwig Klages (1872–1956), German anthropologist; Hans Sachs (1494–1576), German Meistersinger.

8–10. Notes: "Sidelights from Salassi [?]: —The Song of the Birds—Francesco da Milano (16th century)—Gerhart Münch (20th century) [by metamorphosis]—Violin Part— Part 1."

Final ideogram. Chinese seal characters, perhaps a phonetic transcription of Münch's name (*mu-ch'i*). The 1933 date coincides with Pound's organization of music festivals in Rapallo featuring Münch and the violinist Olga Rudge.

CANTO 76

3. "Where memory liveth," from Pound's translation of Cavalcanti's "Donna mi prega."

4. Olivia Rossetti Agresti (1875–1961), daughter of Pre-Raphaelite William Michael Rossetti and broadcaster for Radio Rome, referring to Mussolini.

6. Wife of Amphityron, glimpsed by Odysseus in Hades.

7. Three tree nymphs.

9. Three muses: Walter Savage Landor's Dirce, Sigismundo Malatesta's Isotta, and Cavalcanti's Giovanna, referred to by Dante in the *Vita nuova* as "she who was called Primavera" [i.e. "Spring" or she who will "come first," i.e. before Beatrice].

11–31. Reprise of the visionary encounter on the *salita* (or "hill road") near Sant'Ambrogio recorded in the drafts of Italian Cantos 74–75; cf. **74.445–46**.

13. "On the slope and at the crossing of three roads."

16. "Beneath our cliffs."

19–20. Rapallo lies on the via Aurelia, which runs along the coast from Rome to Pisa to Genoa. The older road ("la vecchia") runs below the church of St. Pantaleone at Sant' Ambrogio. In the drafts of Italian Cantos 74–75, Sigismundo Malatesta and his court poet Basinio are traveling along the via Aurelia toward Genoa when the vision of Cunizza occurs.

21–22. Three apparitions: "Cunizza there at the crossing of three roads,/and the barefoot woman." In the drafts of Italian Cantos 74–75, "la scalza" is a barefoot country woman who suddenly appears halfway up the hill path from Rapallo to Sant'Ambrogio, flee- ing her home that has just been destroyed by bombs and seeking refuge in the church of St. Pantaleone; at **74.446** and **30** below, she declares "I am the Moon." The third apparition here ("and she who said") had also been evoked in the Italian Cantos of Jan.-Feb. 1945: she is Caterina Sforza, Countess of Forlì (1463–1509). Legend has it that while defending the fortress of Ravaldino against the Orsi, she mounted the bat- tlements, defiantly raised her skirts, and boasted that she "had the mould for casting more children."

24–26. "This rotten wind," blowing over the city of Toulouse, north of Mount Ségur, the last stronghold of the heretical Albigensians and believed by Pound (who first visited it in 1919) to be a temple of solar worship or an altar to Mithras, the ancient Persian god of light.

27. Cf. **74.467.**

32. Probably the moldering statue of Diana in the courtyard of Pound's Paris residence, 70 bis rue Notre Dame des Champs.

33. "The times, the times, the mores" (Cf. Cicero's "O Tempora! O Mores!").

34–36. Ralph Cheever Dunning (1865–1930), minor American poet befriended by Pound in Paris in the '20s. The line recalled is, "My garden hath a wall as high/As any wall of Babylon."

40–46. The restaurants of yesteryear.

47. Henri Gauthier-Villars (1859–1931), French popular novelist and literary collaborator of Colette under the pen name "Willy."

49. Pound observed the bric-a-brac of French poet Théophile Gautier (1811–72) in his daughter Judith's apartment in Paris in the '20s.

54. An interior decoration effect produced by placing an electric light behind yellow curtains.

56. "Sloth."

57. Ideogram: *chung¹*, "middle" (also translated by Pound as "pivot," "mean" or "axis").

61. Ideogram: *ch'eng²*, "sincerity," glossed by Pound as: "The precise definition of the word, pictorially the sun's lance coming to rest on the precise spot verbally."

63–65. Two names for Confucius, whom Pound reveres as an historian and anthologist of the *Book of Odes*.

67–78. The quotation from Micah (cf. **74.340**) leads to memories of a synagogue service in Gibraltar witnessed in 1908 (see Canto 12) and allusions to Leviticus and Jeremiah (cf. **74.517–31**).

79–80. Spanish and Italian expressions for "John Doe."

81. I.e. the messianic Zion, or the Temple of Jerusalem.

90. "Before death no whore."

94–101. Memories of Pound's 1912 walking tour through southern France.

102. From Andrew Lang's translation of the medieval French romance *Aucassin and Nicolette*; its hero, Aucassin, asks what he will do in Heaven without his beloved Nicolette by his side.

105. Hans Memling (?1430–95), Flemish painter; Max Elskamp (1862–1931), Belgian Symbolist poet.

107–8. Pound believed (erroneously) that Allied bombing had destroyed the Byzantine Church of St. Nazario Celso in Ravenna, site of the tomb of the Roman empress Galla Placidia (388–450).

112–14. Cf. **74.410.**

115. "Everything indicates that fortune does not last," from a rondeau by Jean Froissart (?1337–?1404), quoted in one of Pound's essays on Arnaut Daniel. Pound's violin sonata, "Hommage à Froissart," was performed in 1926 in Rome.

116–21. Pound had been a tireless promoter of Joyce's *Portrait of an Artist* and *Ulysses* during the teens, but the two men only met for the first time in June 1920 at Lake Garda (cf. **74.79–85**). Such was Joyce's terror of the thunderstorms in the region that he claimed he brought along his son ("fils") Giorgio to act as a lightning conductor.

122. Sara Norton, daughter of the Harvard Dante scholar Charles Eliot Norton; Pound met her in Venice in 1908.

128–35. Evocations of Venice: its Grand Canal; Florian's, the famous café on the Piazza San Marco; *Jorio's Daughter*, a 1904 play by Gabriele D'Annunzio (1863–1938).

136. "The altar on the rostrum."

140. Insulted by an arrogant patrician, the young Mozart challenged him to a battle of snuff-powder, suggesting in the end that the aristocrat could get a better pinch ("prise") by licking his, Mozart's, ass.

143. "To the flowery fountain" (of youth), sought by Ponce de León (?1460–1521) in Florida.

144–46. Aphrodite (whose epithets are given in Latin and Greek, "Kuthêra deina," "powerful [or fearsome] Cythera") appeared in human guise to Anchises, father of Aeneas.

151. "Korê, Delia deina" ("Daughter [Persephone], fearsome Delia/to whom passion is unknown"). The virgin huntress Artemis/Diana, sister of the Delian Apollo.

156. "Polla pathein" ("to suffer much"), cf. *Od.* I, 4: "and his heart experienced many sufferings upon the sea").

160. Cf. **3** above.

162. Cf. **74.496.**

169. DTC provost sergeant so nicknamed because of his habit of ripping all unfastened buttons from trainees' uniforms; a missing button could delay a man's clemency for months.

170–86. Cf. the vision near the cliffs recalled above, **11–31.**

175–76. "And domesticated wild animals." "To the right."

180. I.e. *ittisal* (transliteration from the Arabic), "Union with the divine," a Sufi term used by Avicenna, elsewhere defined by Pound as "contemplation, the identification of the consciousness WITH the object."

181. "Nor [flesh-and-blood?] people."

182. The technical philosophical term "hypostasis" occurs in Pound's commentaries on Cavalcanti's "Donna mi prega" and is defined by the O.E.D. as, "That which subsists, or underlies anything: a) as opposed to qualities, attributes or 'accidents'; b) as distinguished from what is unsubstantial, as a shadow or reflection." Cf. "nec accidens," **74.835.**

182–83. Dione, mother of Aphrodite, sometimes confused with Aphrodite herself. Her planet would therefore be Venus.

184–85. Probably a misprint for Delia (cf. **151** above). Kupris, i.e. Cypris, home of Aphrodite.

189–94. Anecdote related to Pound by his daughter, Mary, who worked in a military hospital in Italy toward the end of the war.

196. "A third heaven," the heaven of Love in *Par.* VIII, 37.

197–202. Cf. **74.79–88.**

203–7. *Time* magazine of August 6: Winston Churchill ("their squeak doll") was swept out of office by the unexpected victory of Clement Atlee's Labour Party; Brendan Bracken was Churchill's minister of information.

209. "I, the writer."

212. Two towns to the north of Pisa. Graf Leopold von Berchtold (1863–1942), warmongering Austro-Hungarian foreign minister (rhymed with Churchill?), visitor to Rapallo.

214. A nereid, wife of Peleus and mother of Achilles.

217. "Are these spirits? [real?] people?"

221. The Kalenda Maya, or May Day fertility rites celebrated by the troubadours, juxtaposed with Aphroditê.

224. A town just south of Rapallo.

229–31. "Hoi barbaroi," the barbarians (i.e. the Allies), whose bombs had damaged the façade of Tempio Malatestiano in Rimini containing images of the "Divine Isotta."

235. "The Loved One: I love." Pound's term of endearment for Olga Rudge.

239. "Periwinkle."

241. "And all that follow."

242. Cf. 74.456.

244. "Dakruôn" ("weeping" or "of tears").

245. "L[aval]. P[étain]. the honest [or honorable] ones." *Time* magazine of August 13 featured a photo of Pierre Laval (1883–1945), former head of the Vichy government, testifying at the trial for treason of Henri Philippe Pétain (1865–1951), chief of state of the collaborationist Vichy regime.

246–47. "I have had pity for others,/probably not enough."

249–50. "Paradise is not artificial/nor is Hell."

251. The East or Southeast Wind. The *Catholic Prayer Book* includes, "Come, Holy Ghost": "O Comforter! to Thee we cry,/Thou heavenly gift of God Most High."

252–53. "The little swineherd." "The fair-tressed goddess" (Circe).

256–310. A mosaic of memories of Venice, from Pound's first arrival in 1908 through the '30s.

256–58. The Campo San Vio runs to the Grand Canal; it was here that Don Carlos, the Bourbon duke of Madrid (1848–1909), lived in 1908; Salviati was a shop where blown glass was sold.

259–63. In 1908, as he was about to publish his first book of poetry, *A Lume Spento* ("With Tapers Quenched"), Pound sat on the bank of the Grand Canal trying to decide whether to throw the proofsheets ("le bozze") into the water or whether to cross to the other side of the canal and deliver his book to the printer—or perhaps simply to wait a day before deciding.

266–67. During the Fascist era, a wooden bridge, Ponte dell'Accademia, replaced the previous iron bridge over the Grand Canal, whose various famous palazzi are enumerated.

268–71. Cf. 74.190. The four marble sirens in the church of Santa Maria dei Miracoli so admired by the guard ("custode") were sculpted by Pietro Lombardo (?1435–1515).

272–73. Near the church of San Giorgio dei Greci is the church of San Giorgio Schiavoni, which contains contains the painting of St. George and the Dragon by Vittore Carpaccio (?1455–?1525).

276. Cf. 74.753.

277. Cf. 74.288. The "abbey" of the Italian painter Italico Brass (1870–1943).

278. "You who pass by this way" (paraphrase of Dante's *Vita nuova*).

280. Katherine Ruth Heyman, a concert pianist for whom Pound acted as an impresario in Venice in 1908.

283. "Don't fight."

286–87. "'Tis adikei" ("who wrongs [you]?"), from Sappho's "Hymn to Aphrodite."

289. Count Giuseppe Volpi (1877–1947), Mussolini's finance minister.

291. 19th President of the U.S. (1877–81).

295. I.e. Sandro Botticelli's painting of Daphne.

297. Churches along the San Trovaso canal.

298–300. Alexander Robertson, firebrand minister of the Scotch Presbyterian Church in Venice.

303–5. In 1908, Pound lived near the confluence of the San Trovaso and Ogni Santi canals, not far from the gondola-yard ("Squero").

307. "Treasure chests."

308–10. Private items in the "hidden nest" Pound shared with Olga Rudge in Venice on the Calle Querini: a painting by the Japanese artist Tami Koumé (Tamijuro Kume [1893–1961]) , a wooden-bound copy of Ovid's *Fasti*, a reproduction of Duccio's bas-relief of Isotta.

311. "Formerly of the Malatestas."

312. A city near Rimini once controlled by the Malatestas, damaged by Allied bombing.

318–19. "Smoothed with tears/polished tears WEEPING."

320. "Out of nothing."

321. "The conch-shell" (that bears Venus ashore).

322. "POIKILOTHRON, ATHANATA" ("richly enthroned, immortal"), opening words of Sappho's hymn to Aphrodite.

324. "Immortal, cruel."

325. Perhaps Antonio Pisano, a painter employed by Sigismundo Malatesta and patronized by Leonello d'Este.

327. Both Arezzo and Cortona have churches featuring paintings by Fra Angelico (? 1440–55).

328. "Poor devils."

330. "Slave against slave."

334. Cf. **74.539**

335. "NESON AMUMONA" ("a noble island"), from *Od.* XII, 261–62, "We came next to a noble island belonging to a god," i.e.Thrinakia, where Odysseus's companions killed the cattle of the Sun.

CANTO 77

4. Cf. **74.625.**

6. An employee of the German consulate in Florence.

8. In 1943, the German government announced that the mass grave of 4,250 Polish officers had been discovered in the forest near Katyn and accused the Soviets of responsibility for their deaths; the latter in turn accused the Germans, but refused to permit an investigation by the International Red Cross (in 1989, Soviet scholars revealed that Stalin had indeed ordered the 1941 massacre).

9. "The upper crust governs."

12. Ideogram: Pound provides a gloss of all the ideograms in this Canto in the "Explication" appended at its end.

18. Confucius.

19–28. An anecdote from Pound's days at Hamilton College in Clinton, New York, 1903–5.

33. "See" Epictetus, Stoic philosopher (fl. 55–135); Publilius Syrus, Roman author of mimes and maxims.

34. Major star in the constellation of Boötes; the "smoke-hole" here and elsewhere is the ventilation opening at the top of Pound's pyramidal army tent.

39. The jealous evil spirit ("hannya") wearing the mask of a female demon with golden eyes and horns in the Noh play *Awoi no uye*, translated by Pound in 1916.

43–47. For "Hooh Fasa" and the city of Wagadu, cf. **74.93, 74.198ff.**

· 48. "(The South Wind is jealous)."

49. "Chthonos," the "earth" out of which the Spartoi rose fully armed to help Cadmus build the city of Thebes.

·50. The four destroyed incarnations of the allegorical city of Wagadu were Dierra (vanity), Agada (falsehood), Ganna (greed), and Silla (dissension).

51. William Brooke Smith, to whom Pound dedicated his first book of poems, *A Lume Spento* (1908).

54. From the *Analects* of Confucius, IX, 30, later translated by Pound: "The flowers of the prunus japonica deflect and turn, do I not think of you dwelling afar? He said: It is not the thought, how can there be distance in that?"

55. "The North Wind." "Kylin," a fabulous Chinese monster.

62. On the Delaware River, near Trenton, c. 1907.

70. In Regent's Park, London.

72. Tami Koumé, cf. **76.308.**

73–75. Cf. T.S. Eliot's 1918 poem "Whispers of Immortality."

79. "Psucharion ei bastazon nekron" ("you are a tiny soul supporting a corpse"), attributed to the stoic philosopher Epictectus.

82. Allusion to the erotico-religious dancing of Serafina Astafeiva (1876–1934), the "Grishkin" of Eliot's poem, here associated with Theodora, wife of the Byzantine emperor Justinian (483–565). Cf. **79.16.**

83. José Maria de Elizondo, Spanish priest who facilitated Pound's research in Spain in 1906. Cf. **81.9.**

85. "The ship [or bird] carried one of them away," from the Anglo-Saxon poem *The Wanderer*.

88–90. The religious festivities on the day of Corpus Christi, as exemplified by the ceremonial game-playing and dancing in the medieval church of Auxerre in southern France, described by G.R.S. Mead in the journal *The Quest* (1912).

91–92. I.e. "shithouse." Japan signed the armistice on August 14, 1945.

94. Ida, the mountain where Anchises and Aphrodite "kalliplokama" ("with beautiful locks of hair") were married.

95. Cf. **74.462.**

97. The port in Sicily where, according to Pound, sailors still told yarns from the *Odyssey*.

99. The "seven words" may be those that close Pound's 1915 poem "Dum Capitolium Scandet": "Clear speakers, naked in the sun, untrammelled."

100. Cf. Horace, *Odes III*, xxx.7–9: "usque ego postera crescam laude recens, dum Capitolium scandet cum tacita virgine pontifex" ("I shall arise with fresh praise in the future, as long as the high priest climbs the Capitoline Hill with silent virgins").

101. The atomic bomb was dropped on Hiroshima on August 6, 1945.

103. The splitting of the atom (described in *Time* magazine, August 13) here juxtaposed with the inscribed seals or (bamboo) tally sticks of Chinese tradition—which, like the Greek *symbolon*, were broken in half (right through a line of characters) to be later rejoined as a visible guarantee of trust or mutual contract. *Mencius* IV, II, 1.

104–5. Legendary emperors of China ("the Middle Kingdom"), separated by a millennium.

110. "Direction of the will," from Dante's *De Vulgari Eloquentia.*

112. Byron observed "In morals, I prefer Confucius to the Ten Commandments, and Socrates to St. Paul."

115–16. Voltaire's history, *The Century of Louis XIV* (1751), concludes with a section contrasting the traditional religious tolerance of China with the bigotry of the West, just as the Usura of Cantos 47–51 segues into the China of Cantos 52–61.

117–18. In 1766 B.C., the Chinese emperor Ch'eng T'ang opened a copper mine and issued money so the people could buy grain.

120. Cf. **74.161.**

121–22. One of the Seven Sages, Thales demonstrated how a philosopher could easily make money by investing in olive crop futures (as reported by Aristotle). The Monte dei Pasci bank of Siena was Pound's model financial institution, issuing credit at low interest backed by the common agricultural wealth of Tuscany.

123. Thomas Jefferson's maxim.

125–27. A recurring theme: banks create money *ex nihilo*, on which they charge interest. "Buggering" replaced by "b. . . . . . ." in 1949 Faber edition.

129. Cf. **76.334.**

132. "Cythera" (Aphrodite).

133–34. "Hupo chthonos" ("under the earth"). "Gea" ("earth"). Cf. **49** above.

138–41. Confucian slogans (a number of which Pound had printed up as poster strips in the '40s to be pasted on the walls of Rapallo).

144. Roman goddess of the earth ("gea"), the shape of whose ample breasts Pound sees incarnated by two mountains in the Apuan range north of Pisa.

145–46. The Italian dramatist Luigi Pirandello (1867–1936) expressing fears about Jean Cocteau's modern stage adaptation of the Oedipus story.

147–48. More restaurants.

149. The Vorticist sculptor Henri Gaudier-Brzeska (1892–1915) sizing up the considerable girth of the American poet Amy Lowell (1874–1925) at a dinner at Dieudonné's in London in 1914.

150. Cf. **74.419.**

153. Classmate of Pound's at U. Penn. (1902–3) and author of a doctoral dissertation on Heraclitus and Parmenides.

154–63. Anecdotes relating to the Japanese dancer Michio Ito (c. 1892–1961), who performed in Yeats's play *At the Hawk's Well* in 1916.

164–69. The full couplet of this G.I. song in Provençal "rimas escarsas" ("rare rhymes") runs, "My gal's got great big tits/Just like Jack Dempsey's mitts" (sung to the tune of "My gal's a corker/She's a real New Yorker").

171. After his release from three weeks in the "gorilla cage."

172. "Beautiful bosom." "Demeter," "she who copulates" (an epithet of Venus in the *Pervigilium Veneris*).

175. The Pisan purgatory compared to the slaves' Middle Passage between Africa and the New World.

177. Conte Galeazzo Ciano de Cortelazzo (1903–44), Mussolini's son-in-law, influential member (and Pound was convinced, betrayer) of his regime.

182. Felice Chilanti (1914–), dissident anarcho-Fascist and friend of Pound's, arrested and imprisoned in 1941–42 for plotting against Mussolini's government.

183–87. Misrule in Gais (Italian Tyrol), where Pound's daughter Mary was raised. The empty valise placed at the military monument at Bruneck was the Tyrol's way of telling the Italians it was time to pack up and leave.

195. John Hersey's A *Bell for Adano* (1944)?

196. Alice and Edmund Dulac, friends of Pound in London, c. 1914.

199. "Kai Ida, thea" ("and Ida, goddess").

200. Isa Miranda (1909–82), famous Italian star of stage and screen, best known for her roles in Max Ophuls' *La Signora di Tutti* (1934) and *Scipio Africanus* (1936), produced by Mussolini's son Vittorio.

207. "Hule" ("matter," here "shit").

211. Childhood friend of Pound's daughter.

213–19. Margaret Cravens (1881–1912), early friend and patron of Pound's and a descendant of the American poet Sidney Lanier (1842–81); her grandmother, Rose O'Neale, a Confederate spy known as "Rebel Rose," drowned while trying to deliver gold from England to Jefferson Davis. As in the Greek tragedy of the House of Atreus, her grandmother's accidental death and her father's suicide were repeated when Margaret Cravens took her own life in 1912, and thus "entered the lotus."

225–26. "They do not exist, their surroundings confer on them/an existence."

227. Pound was quite attracted to the mystical doctrines of Emmanuel Swedenborg (1668–1772) in his early years. The three spheres are the natural, the spiritual, and the celestial.

230. Cf. **74.131.**

231. Cf. **74.842.**

233–45. Henri-Martin Barzun (1881–1973), a 1912 proponent of *simultanéiste* poetry, which involved the visual scoring (or even phonographic recording) of several voices at once. Abbé Jean Rousselot (1846–1924), a pioneer in experimental phonetics who recorded the *vers libre* poetry of André Spire (1868–1966), Robert de Souza (1865–1946), and Pound in order to determine its rhythmic features. His acoustical research apparently led to the development of sonar.

246–48. "'A priest in disguise . . . Strikes me as a priest in disguise' At the door/'Don't know, Sir, but he strikes me as a priest in disguise." In reference to Jacques Maritain (1882–1973), French neo-Thomist philosopher. "Maritain" replaced by "M . . . ." in 1949 Faber edition.

251–53. Salon gossip: The Countess de Rohan (whose family motto is quoted below at 258) opining that the arch-conservative Léon Daudet (1867–1942) would certainly block Jean Cocteau's election to the prestigious Académie Goncourt.

254–57. Electoral corruption in the U.S.: "Alf" Landon and Wendell Willkie, Republican nominees for the presidency in 1936 and 1940.

258–59. "[Since] I am not the king, I do not deign to be the prince," Rohan family motto, quoted by Mussolini when declining an aristocratic title offered to him by the king (though he did agree to be awarded honorary citizenship by the city of Florence).

262. "With great disdain," *Inf.* X, 36, describing the scornful pride of Farinata degli Uberti.

264. Cf. **74.90.**

266–67. Francesco del Cossa (fl. 1435–77) painted the frescoes celebrating the months of spring in the Schifanoia palace in Ferrara. Posts in the shape of gibbets lined the perimeter of the DTC stockade.

269. Cf. **74.171.**

276. "Fleeing Rome into the land of the Sabines."

277–80. Pound's visitors in the '20s and '30s: James Joyce (in Sirmione), and the British economist Arthur Kitson (1860–1937) and William Butler Yeats (in Rapallo).

284–85. Basil Bunting, another frequent visitor of Pound's in Rapallo, translated portions of the Persian epic *Shah Namah* by Firdausi (c. 940–1020), whose name, inscribed on Bunting's door, is given here in Persian script.

287. Pound cotranslated some of the poems of the Indian sage Kabir (1400–50) in 1913, around the same time he was promoting (with Yeats) the poetry of Rabindranath Tagore (1861–1941).

291–95 Cf. **74.36.** "Money lender" (Hindi).

301. The Kohinoor, India's most famous diamond, was among the British Empire's crown jewels.

304. Cf. **74.64.**

307–8. German headquarters in the Roman suburb of Frascati were bombed the very day Italy signed an armistice on September 8, 1943.

310. "The banking business."

311. Popular American song (heard over the DTC loudspeakers?).

313–14. Cf. **266** above. According to Yeats (who had it from Pound), the Schifanoia frescoes provided one of the structural models for the Cantos: The lower panel represents scenes from the court life of Borso D'Este (the domain of the "casual" or "quotidian"); the middle panel contains the signs of the zodiac (here, the Ram and Bull constellations, symbolizing the domain of the "recurrent"); the upper panel depicts the triumphs of the gods (the domain of the "eternal").

318. Trojan prophetess who predicted the destruction of the city when Helen came to Troy; rescued by Agamemnon when the city fell, she was murdered with him by his wife Clytaemenestra upon his return to Mycenae.

320–21. "My sister, my sister,/who danced on a sequin [i.e. a gold coin]."

324. Cult name of Dionysus.

CANTO 78

1. Cf. **77.94.**

4. "Peace of the world," an allusion to the forty or so nations (or "geese"?) gathered at the San Francisco Peace Conference in the summer of 1945?

5. Cf. **77.319–20.** Here, as elsewhere, the "little sister" may be the moon.

6. Cf. **77.318.**

16. Cf. **77.166–67.**

18. In some of the New Directions printings of the *Cantos* of the 1980s, its publisher, James Laughlin, here inserted a line from one of Pound's postcards which referred to the former's tendency to sacrifice business for the pleasure of skiing: "(And the Jaz slidin' down Pike's Peak on a tea tray)." The interpolation was subsequently removed.

19. "Thrice mournfully: Itys" (Horace, *Odes* IV. xii.5). Cf. Canto 4: Procne killed her son Itys and had him cooked and fed to Tereus upon discovering that the latter had raped her sister Philomena and cut out her tongue so that she could not divulge his crime. Transformed into a nightingale, Philomena mournfully calls out the name of the unfortunate Itys.

20. "Two-faced Janus" (a pun on Count Ciano/Giano, cf. **77.177**?).

26–27. Alfred Moritz Mond (1863–1930), English industrialist, chairman of Imperial Chemical Industries.

29–33. Cosimo de' Medici (1389–1484) kept a red notebook containing details of debts to be called in; Lorenzo de' Medici (1449–92) traveled to Naples to arrange peace with King Ferrante. Cf. Canto 21.

34–35. "Abandoned to the earth." Pietro Metastasio (1698–1782), author of the libretto for the opera *Dido Abandoned* (1724).

36–41. "The Program of Verona," a manifesto written by Mussolini outlining the policies of his new Salò Republic (headquartered on Lake Garda, near Sirmio and Gardone). The 1943 Verona Program, socialist in inspiration, underscored "the rights *to* ("alla") not the rights *of* ("della") property."

42. The piazza San Sepulchro in Milan, where Mussolini launched his political career.

44. "Faith."

47. Carl Goedel, translator and broadcaster for the Ministry of Popular Culture, which sponsored Pound's wartime radio broadcasts; subsequently a member of the propaganda bureau of the Salò Republic.

48. Both Dionysus and Theseus passed through the island of Naxos on their respective ways home. The following lines evoke incidents from Pound's 450-mile trek from Rome to his daughter's village of Gais in the Italian Tyrol in September 1943, after the fall of Mussolini—an odyssey rhymed in lines **61–66** below with Aeneas's journey from Ilium to Latium in order to found the eternal city of Rome (or, as in line **42** above, "to dream the Republic").

53–59. "Soup." "The knapsack." "Camp bed." "God bless." "The Master!" "Pappa has come."

61. Cf. **77.276**.

62–66. The opening of the *Aeneid*, in the Scots translation by Gawin Douglas (1553) prized by Pound.

67. Cf. **74.340**.

69–71. Henri Gaudier-Brzeska, cf. **77.149**. Thomas Ernest Hulme (1883–1917), English philosopher and poet, author of the poem "Mana aboda." Percy Wyndham Lewis (1882–1957), English writer and painter, coeditor (with Pound and Gaudier-Brzeska) of the Vorticist magazine *Blast* (1914).

73. Lt. Col. John Lincoln Steele (1911–94), commanding officer of the DTC.

81. Pallas Athena. "Dikê," justice.

84–86. Fascist dicta: "We are tired of a government in which there is no responsible person having a front name, a hind name and address." "Liberty is not a right but a duty" (Pound had the latter printed on his stationery).

88. "Present!" standard reply to the roll call at Fascist gatherings

89. "Gave shit to" (followed by an enumeration of Mussolini's accomplishments in Abyssinia and economic reforms).

93–95. Cf. **74.419**.

96–97. Cf. **74.614**.

98–99. Wise emperors: Justinian (cf. **77.82**), Titus Flavius Vespasianus (9–79), and Antoninus Pius (86–161), who decreed that international maritime law ("the law of Rhodes") rather than Roman law be observed at sea.

102. M.I. Rostovtzeff (1870–1952), author of *Social and Economic History of the Hellenistic World* (1941).

105–6. "Duke Wang of T'ang," title of Book III of *The Works of Mencius*, which recommends variable rather than fixed taxes on grain, depending on the harvest.

107–9. "Cricket." "Fifteenth-century."

110–14. "It is sometimes said in the village/that a helmet serves no purpose/none at all/ It serves only to give courage/to those who have none at all" (French folk song).

115. The reopening of the annual Mozart festival in Salzburg, Austria, was mentioned in *Time*, August 27.

116–17. "Here sings Wolfgang the cricket/Piano [softly], the bass viol."

120–22. Writers encountered by Pound in Paris in 1913: Laurent Tailhade (1854–1919), French satirical poet; "Willy" (cf. **76.47**); Albert Mockel (1866–1945), editor of the Belgian Symbolist magazine, *La Wallonie*, which published the poem "Ballet" by the Franco-American Symbolist Stuart Merrill (1863–1915), a line of which is here quoted: "the buffoons in their pink crystal helmets."

123–25. Restaurants, cf. **74.286**.

128–31. Cf. **74.796**. In 1911 Pound visited San Zeno with William Carlos Williams's brother, Edgar, who made the remark on modern mass-produced columns.

132–33. Farinata degli Uberti, 13th-century leader of the Ghibelline faction of Florence, ancestor of Ubaldo degli Uberti (1881–1945), Italian admiral and friend of Pound's.

134. Can Grande della Scala (1291–1329), friend and protector of Dante, his face on the equestrian statue at his tomb in Verona evoking a boyhood acquaintance of Pound's.

135. Touchstone Cavalcanti line. Cf. **74.687, 74.799**.

137–42. In the summer of 1922 Pound met with T.S. Eliot ("the decadent one") and Evelyn St. Bride Scratton (1883–1964), whom he affectionately referred to as "Thiy," in the Caffè Dante near the arena in Verona to discuss the editorial program of Eliot's new journal, *The Criterion*.

143–45. Arthur Griffith (1872–1922), Irish founder of Sinn Fein, in conversation with Pound in 1921.

146. Cf. **74.725**.

147–50. From the *Analects* XII, 21–22, later translated by Pound: "Fan Chi'ih walking with him [i.e. Confucius] below the rain altars (or to celebration of the rain sacrifice pantomime) said: Venture to ask how to lift one's conscience in action; to correct the hidden tare, and separate one's errors? He said: An excellent question!"

152–62. 1919: U.S. Senate opposition to the League of Nations and passage of the 18th Amendment, prohibiting the manufacture and sale of intoxicating liquors (represented by Bacchus, god of wine). Senators Henry Cabot Lodge (1850–1954) and Philander Chase Knox (1853–1921), opponents (like Pound) of the League of Nations. Rep. George Tinkham, Massachusetts isolationist, cf. **74.288**.

163. Odon Por's *Politica economico-sociale in Italia*, translated by Pound in 1941.

165. Cf. **76.334**.

166. Cf. **74.40**.

171. Ideogram: *tao⁴*, "process, way."

174. Cf. **74.552**.

175–78. "In this matter." Refers to Mussolini and the manner and causes of his death. Cf. **74.5**.

179. Title of a medieval Arabic romance, translated by Wilfrid Scawen Blunt (cf. **81.169**), in which the theft of a mare provided the cause of wars ("causus bellorum"). For "mits," cf. **77.164**.

180–82. The *Memoirs of Harriette Wilson* (1789–1846) relate a discussion with the Duke of Wellington concerning the propriety of a man having sex with his boots on.

188. "Manners," in Gawin Douglas's Scots spelling (cf. **62** above). "He saw [the many manners of men] and cities," from Andreas Divus's Latin translation of *Od*. I, 2. "Polumetis" ("many-witted"), Homeric epithet for Odysseus.

189. The French translator Hugues Salel's 1543 version of the *Odyssey* referred to him as "this shrewd character." "Otis" echoes "Ou Tis" (cf. **74.23**), while also referring to James Otis (1725–83), author of one of the earliest works on Greek prosody in colonial America.

189–94. Encountered on the beach by Odysseus in Book VI of the *Odyssey*, after she had finished washing the household linen and here juxtaposed with a modern Nausicaa in Bagno di Romagna, a town in northern Italy.

195. Cf. **6** above.

197. In the *Odyssey*, asphodels are the flowers of oblivion and death.

201. Spanish playwright (1562–1635), about whom Pound planned to write a doctoral dissertation under Professor Hugo Rennert of the University of Pennsylvania.

203–4. "There is no love without jealousy/Without secrecy there is no love" (the latter line the title of a Lope de Vega play edited by Rennert).

205. "The madwoman," Dona Juana (1479–1555), daughter of Ferdinand of Aragon and Isabella of Castile, driven mad by her jealousy of her unfaithful husband, Philip.

206. Cf. **74.445** and **76.11–31**.

210. "Three woman around my mind," echoes Dante's *Rime*, 47, "Tre donne intorno al cor mi son venute" ("Three ladies have come around my heart"), where the female figures are traditionally interpreted as the three incarnations of Justice. Three tree nymphs, three muses, and three apparitions—Cunizza, "the bare-footed woman," and Caterina Sforza—appear in the vision of **76.6–21**, recalled four lines above. More specifically biographical interpretations (involving Dorothy Pound and Olga Rudge as two of the women) have also been proposed.

212. Cf. **76.4**.

217–19. William Carlos Williams (1883–1963), Pound's fellow student at the University of Pennsylvania, whose "Spring and All" contains the celebrated lines: "so much depends/upon/a red wheel/barrow/glazed with rain/water/beside the white chickens."

222–28. *Spring and Autumn Annals*, a chronological record (by Confucius) of the chief events in the state of Lu between 722 and 484 B.C. and the last of the Five Classics. The quotation is from *Mencius* VII, 2, ii.

CANTO 79

1. The Baptistery near the Leaning Tower of Pisa, visible from the DTC.

3. Cf. **77.266**.

4–7. Cf. "I could not love thee, Dear, so much,/Loved I not Honor more," from "To Lucasta, Going to the Wars" by Richard Lovelace (1618–58), included in Speare's *Pocket Book of Verse* (cf. **80.664**).

10. From a famous aria by 17th-century composer Giulio Caccini ("Amarili mia bella").

14. The "theatre" of Salzburg, hence "she" is probably Mozart's wife.

16. Serafima Astafieva, Russian dancer and director of a ballet school in London (cf. **77.73**). Wigmore Gallery, Marylebone, London.

19. German WWII tune, popular with the Allied and Axis troops.

24–29. Survivors: Goedel, cf. **78.47**; Giorgio Paresce (1900–82), Pound's supervisor at the Italian Ministry of Popular Culture. The death sentence of Pétain for treason (cf. **76.245**) was commuted to life imprisonment by a vote of 14 to 13, as reported in *Time*, August 27. "Où sont," from Villon's "Where are [the snows of yesteryear]?"

30–33. Scott, Whiteside (and Mr. Allingham below), trainees at the DTC.

39. Famous piano make.

43–45. Cf. **78.109.** Cosimo Tura (?1430–95) also contributed frescoes to the Schifanoia Palace in Ferrara.

56. "Roman fort."

57. Paraphrase of the end of Book I of Caesar's *Gallic Wars*.

59. Guards on horseback patrolling the circuit of the drill field where the military band (cf. the "bumm drum" above) is playing.

61. Jannequin, cf. Canto 75; Orzio Vechii (?1550–1605), Italian composer; Il Bronzino (1502–72), Italian painter at the court of Cosimo I.

62–65. Two Noh plays, contrasted with the "rascality" of Odysseus's attack on Ismarus soon after he left Troy ("Troas"), a rash act which so angered the gods that they delayed his return home by ten years (*Od.* IX, 39).

70–73. Ideograms: *tz'u²* ("words, speech, message") and *ta ²* ("to apprehend"), translated by Pound as "Get the meaning across. Stop." "E poi basta" ("and then enough").

76. Guido d'Arezzo (fl.1000–50), Italian composer who developed the modern system of musical notation known as the Hexacord (five lines to a staff). See **105** below.

78. "Most fragrant fresh rose," from a poem by Ciullo d'Alcamo (fl. 1230–50).

80. Edmond Goncourt (1822–96) and Jules Goncourt (1830–70) express their contempt for the French Revolution in their *Journal* , December 21, 1866.

83–85. American flag with Ugolino's tower (cf. **74.379**) and a Pisan church in the distance.

90–95. The economic theme: Clement Attlee (1883–1967), new head of Britain's ruling Labour Party, proposed nationalizing the Bank of England in 1945. James Ramsey MacDonald (1866–1937), British Labour Party leader who switched sides to the Conservatives in the '30s. "Leave the Duke, go for the gold," a quote from Canto 50 in reference to cornering the gold market and creating a run on the banks in 1832 England. "In less than a geological epoch," H. L. Mencken to Pound, about the slowness of the public to respond to proposals for monetary reform. John Wilkes (1727–97), the Lord Mayor of London who fixed the price of bread to benefit the poor.

96. "Ethos," moral aim.

97–99. Attributes of the goddess Athena: gray eyes ("caesia oculi"), or rather intermittently "glinting" ("glaux") eyes. In *Patria Mia* (1913), Pound describes Pallas Athena as "the much pitied intellectual," in contrast to Aphrodite ("enough said").

101. "And then?"

108. "Chatterer." The Chinese characters, *huang² niao³ chih³*, read "yellow bird rests" (from the Confucian *Book of Odes* 230).

109–10. The author ("auctor") had by now spent three months imprisoned at Pisa.

111. Cf. **77.144** (and **116–17** below).

112. "As if he held Hell in great disdain," *Inf.* X, 36. Cf. **77.261**

114. One of the Seven against Thebes who defied Zeus by attempting to scale the wall.

129–31. W.B. Yeats's aristocratic "mockery of a time/Half dead at the top" (in "Blood and the Moon") and of "this pragmatic pig of a world."

132. The Youanmi Gold Mines, Ltd.

135. William Keith (1838–1911), American painter; Donatello (?1386–1466), Italian sculptor, best known for his statue of David.

136. Sacred to the wine-god Dionysus and traditional emblem of keen-sightedness, the lynx figured in the private feline mythology Pound shared with his wife, Dorothy, for whose birthday (September 14) he composed the choruses of this Canto.

140. Algonquin Indian name for the power that suffuses all things.

141. From Firdausi's *Shah nameh*? Cf. **77.285.**

144. Circe instructing Odysseus to descend into the Underworld (*Od*. X, 450).

149–60. Lydia Yavorska, a/k/a Princess Bariatinsky (1874–1921), Russian-born actress and acquaintence of Pound's in London. "Dear Master."

161. "Eni Troiê" ("in Troy"), from the song the sirens ("fish-tails") sing in *Od*. XII, 189.

165. Pound was known at the DTC as "Uncle Ez." This is the only appearance of his name in *The Pisan Cantos*.

166. The Morning and Evening stars.

167–72. "Silenus," companion of Dionysus. "Casey," corporal at the DTC. "Bassarids," Thracian maenads. "Maelids," apple nymphs ("my one bit of personal property in greek mythology").

176. John Calhoun (1782–1850), senator from South Carolina, champion of the Confederate cause.

183. God of fertility, son of of Dionysus and Aphrodite; "Iakchos, Io! Cythera, Io!" ("Hail Dionysus! Hail Aphrodite").

192. "Lord, have mercy."

198. Cf. **16** above.

201. Species of small insects devastating to grape crops.

202. "Iakche, Iakche, Chaire " ("Dionysus, Dionysus, Hail"). "AOI," cf. **81.94.**

203. Because Persephone (also known as "Kore," the "daughter" of Demeter) ate the pomegranate seed that Dis gave her, Zeus condemned her to return to Hades for four months each year.

210. Roman goddess of fruit trees.

219. Daughters of Helios, the sun.

223. "Rattlesnake's rattle, castanet."

231. "Glaukopis" ("glare-eyed"), Homeric eptithet for Athena; cf. **97** above.

237. "*Ichôr*," the juice that courses in the veins of gods.

240–43. Alludes to the three nights of festivities evoked in the *Pervigilium Veneris*, the feast of Venus Genetrix, whose May Day rites Pound located at the source of troubadour song.

261–81. "Aphrodite." "Helios." "Deina ei, Cythera" ("You are fearsome, Cythera [Aphrodite]"). "Korê kai Dêlia kai Maia" ("Kore [the daughter] and Delia [Artemis/Diana] and Maia [mother of Hermes]"). "Threefold [i.e. in Trinity] as prelude." "Cyprus Aphroditê." "Cythera." "The grove needs an altar." "C[h]imbica," a South American puma and, according to W.H. Hudson, "friend of man, the most loyal of wildcats."

CANTO 80

4. "Themis," law.

5. "I love therefore I am" (A French version of this axiom, "J'ayme donc je suis" was printed on Pound's St. Elizabeths stationery).

6. Margot Asquith (1864–1945), wife of the British prime minister and *enfant terrible* of London society, whose passing was noted in *Time* magazine, August 6.

7–12. Walter Morse Rummel (1887–1953), composer and pianist (apparently admired by Debussy), here remembered in his Paris apartment, with polar bear rug and Estonian (not Finnish) wife. Pound stayed at Rummel's flat in Paris 1911–12, hence the allusions to breakfast croissants, *pains au lait* ("milk rolls"), and Gervais cheese.

14. Cf. **74.**373 and **244** below.

15. "Eat bread, boy!"

18–19. "I grow old, but I love." Cf. **83.**205.

16–31. Memories of Madrid 1906: "Las Meninas," a painting by Velázquez, followed by other works viewed at the Prado Museum. "Las Américas," a bazaar in Madrid.

34–36. British critic Arthur Symons (1865–1945) remembering his meetings with the French Symbolist poet Paul Verlaine; French critic Léon Hennique (1851–1935) remembering the novelist Gustave Flaubert (1821–80), friend of the Russian novelist Ivan Turgenev (1818–83).

38. Misremembered Greek: "aglaos alaou pornê Persephoneia" ("bright Persephone has granted reason to the blind man," *Od.* X, 490).

39. In Canto 47, Tiresias (consulted by Odysseus in Hades in *Od.* XI) is described as "who even dead, yet hath his mind entire!"

44–46. Vidkun Quisling (1887–1945), Norwegian Fascist leader, whose trial for treason opened on August 20, 1945.

53–54. Pétain (cf. **79.**28), military hero of the victory over the Germans at Verdun (1916); Léon Blum, leader of France's socialist Popular Front governement (1936–40) testified at Pétain's trial, accusing him of treason (*Time* magazine, August 6). Line 54 deleted in the 1949 Faber edition.

62. "Plain in her neatness" (Horace, *Odes* I.v.5).

64. James Legge (1815–97), editor of the 7-volume translation of *The Chinese Classics* (1861–86). Pound had the 1923 edition of Legge's *The Four Books* [the *Analects*, the *Great Learning*, the *Doctrine of the Mean*, and *Mencius*] with him at Pisa.

66–74. Tzu Hsi, empress dowager and ruler of China, 1898–1908. Confucius's visit to the somewhat disreputable duchess Nan-tze mentioned in *Analects* VI evokes the name of the shipping heiress Nancy Cunard (1896–1965), who had a house in southern France.

75–90. American poets: Sadakichi Hartmann (1867–1944); Richard Hovey (1864–1900); Trumbull Stickney (1874–1904); Frederic Wadsworth Loring (1848–71); George Santayana (1863–1952); Bliss Carman (1861–1929) [Canadian]; Walt Whitman (1819–92).

94. Petri Nenni (1891–1980), head of the Italian Socialist Party, prominent member of Italian governments after Mussolini's ouster in 1943.

95–96. Cf. **74.**17, for the disciples' problems of "regrouping" after the death of Confucius.

97–111. Mussolini betrayed.

112–28. William Butler Yeats, remembered by his 1899 line "Tread softly because you tread on my dreams," was a member of the Irish senate, 1922–28. Padraic Colum (1881–1972), Irish poet, author of the lines "O woman, shapely as the swan,/On your account I shall not die."

129–47. Memories of Siena: The Palio, annual August 15th horse race in which the 17 districts ("contrade") of the city (such as "Torre" and "Civetta") compete against each other, involving a ceremonial float ("carrochio") and a parade of local flags and banners representing the traditional city guilds ("arti"). "Gribizzi," fancies. "Where is Barilli?" (Italian music critic of the 1930s). "Calvario," cavalry. "Prete," priest. Phrases in Sienese pronunciation: "It's not a district, it's a complex." "Chamomile of the field." "Osservanza," a church outside Siena containing Della Robbia terra cotta enamels damaged by Allied bombing—as was the façade of Malatesta's Tempio in Rimini.

148–53. Cf. **78.** 25; **79.**92; **74.**164.

160–76. Thomas Lovell Beddoes (1803–49), English author of the verse drama, *Death's Jest Book* (1850), which speaks of the ancient rabbinical doctrine of *luz*, a seed-shaped bone believed to be the only portion of the body which resists decomposition after death and hence provides a literal guarantee of immortality and possible resurrection (a doctrine denied by the rival Jewish sect of the Sadducees). Here juxtaposed with T.S. Eliot's *Ash Wednesday*: "And God said/Shall these bones live? shall these/Bones live?" and with the Shakespearian tag from *The Waste Land*, "Those are pearls that were his eyes."

178. "Cross of Malta, figure of the sun," markings on Pound's talismanic eucalyptus nib, his mnemonic *luz*. Cf. **14** above. Ideograms: "How is it far?" Cf. **77.**54.

180. The chants of the trainees doing forced drills late in the evening?

202. From "The Battle Hymn of the Republic."

211–14. "Bygone days" (Horace, *Ars poetica*); "OU TIS" ("no man"). "Achronos" ("without (or beyond) time").

216–25. "P.c.," postcard. "Perkeo's tub," the Great Vat of Heidelberg. Ideogram: ch'uan³, or "dog" (including the character for "man" and evoking the dog star Sirius near the constellation Orion).

229–230. *Analects* XIV,18.

233–35. "But/thus I descended through the malignant air" (*Inf.* V,1). "One must take the weather [or time] as it comes," from a rondeau by Froissart.

242–45. Pound left America in 1908, his first stop Gibraltar; he left England in 1920 (with a letter from Hardy concerning the title of his 1919 poem "Homage to Sextus Propertius"); he was seized by Italian partisans at Sant'Ambrogio on May 3, 1945.

247–52. Associated the Italian Cantos of Jan.-Feb. 1945, which recount a meeting with "la scalza" on the hill path below Sant'Ambrogio; cf. **76.**22. In one of the drafts, the peasant woman sits by her dead son, here evoked in Ezraic Italian: "At St. Bartholomew's I saw myself [or I met] with the little boy,/Who was nailed to the ground with his arms spread/in the form of a Gemistus [i.e. Maltese?] cross. She said: 'I am the moon.'/With her feet on the silver scythe/she seemed to me of pitiful appearance."

253–54. Alexandre Dumas (1824–95), author of *La Dame aux camélias* (1852), remembered by Pound as having said: "Je pleure parce que j'ai des larmes."

256. "Seeds of motion," cf. *luz* above.

260–63. Cf. **74.**180.

264. Venus brought ashore on a seashell ("nautile").

270. Diana of Ephesus, patron of silversmiths.

273–74. "And in Mount Joy," Italian place name evocative of the town of Allègre ("joyous") in southern France where Pound witnessed larks rising in 1912.

275–77. "Selfish Aphrodite." Actaeon, victim of the huntress Diana/Artemis (cf. Canto 4). "Be in me as the eternal moods" (from Pound's 1912 poem "Δώρια").

278–79. A town belonging to the Malatestas. Cf. **76.311.**

280. I.e. *wen²*, "literature; literary accomplishement; polite studies," sometimes translated by Pound as "the precise knowledge." "Charites."

285–86. A pun on "adieu," thus "Farewell, Piccadilly, Farewell Leicester Square" (as in the WWII song, "Farewell, Tipperary"), introducing memories of London.

289–305. Owner of Bellotti's Ristorante Italiano in London, who managed to acquire the makings for the Milanese rice dish "risotto" during WWI, and who remembers his poor tippers, as well as anecdotes about the philanderings of the future Edward VII ("the Caressor"). Shakespeare's statue on Leiscester Square bears the inscription from the clown's speech in *Twelfth Night*, IV, ii, "there is no darkness but ignorance," a line left out of Dr. Johnson's 1765 edition of the plays. "The evil that men do," from Shakespeare's *Julius Caesar* III, ii.

307–22. Anecdotes relating to Horace de Vere Cole (1874–1935), friend of the English painter Augustus John and said to be England's most eminent practical joker and lineal descendent of Old King Cole.

327. Achille Ratti (1857–1939), later Pope Pius XI.

329. Catharginian generals.

338. "Priest."

339–40. Ixion, condemned to eternal torment on a spoked wheel in hell because he had courted Hera, wife of Zeus; "Tranacria," ancient Greek name for Sicily, where Vulcan solved the problem of perpetual motion by a wheel with three spokes, the heraldic emblem of the Isle of Man.

341–53. George Sauter, Bavarian portrait painter living in London, associate of James McNeill Whistler (1834–1903). Otto von Bismark (1815–98), Helmuth Von Moltke (1800–91), Prussian military figures. The Boer War (1899–1902) pitted England against South Africa. Pablo Sarasate (1844–1908), Spanish violinist and subject of Whistler's portrait *Arrangement in Black*. Eugene Ysaÿe (1858–1931), Belgian violinist.

356. Albert Leber, a confectioner in Kensington, London (where Pound lived in a court off Church Street,1909–14).

362. "Unable to unroot [myself]."

363–76. Memories of a 1919 visit to Toulouse at the home of the father of Edmund Dulac (1882–1953), French illustrator and friend of Pound's in London.

382. "My compliments." The Vorticist sculptor Henri Gaudier-Brzeska later enlisted in the French army and died on the front in June 1915.

388. "Good soup makes good soldiers."

391. Arnold Dolmetsch (1858–1940), pioneer of the Early Music movement and maker of renaissance stringed and key instruments.

395. "He's as good as bread." Cf. **78.120.**

398. Pound was foreign editor of the *Dial* magazine in 1920–21, when Gluck's opera *Iphigénie en Tauride* (1779) was performed at his friend Mockel's residence in Paris.

400. "Customs change and the pain remains," an echo of Froissart's "Le corps s'en va, mais le coeur vous demeure," introducing memories of Paris 1912–24.

401. Cf. **78.121.**

402–6. Cf. **74.362; 76.48.**

410. "It's called a garret," allusion to Théophile Gautier's 1872 poem "La Mansarde."

411–31. Natalie Clifford Barney (1876–1972), American expatriate and salon hostess at her elegant townhouse on the rue Jacob, whose garden featured a small Doric temple inscribed with the motto "A l'Amitié" ("To Friendship"). It was at one of her gatherings that Pound met Jean Cocteau ("M. Jean"), whose housekeeper's comments are quoted at **77.246.** Miss Barney received Pound and the American publisher Horace Liveright (1883–1933) at her home around Christmas, 1921. Translations: "hoodlum," "you are very ill-mannered," "See, she's telling you so," "the man with the wooden leg," "Come in, please come in,/everybody's welcome here."

435–38. "These are the customs of Lutetia," from the Latin name for Paris, Lutetia Parisiorum; the Roman arena (or "Roman theatre") of Cluny became the site of a museum of medieval and renaissance antiquities.

439–40. William Butler Yeats's translation of Ronsard's sonnet "Quand vous serez bien vieille" ("When you are old and gray").

441. A 1912 portrait of Pound by Eugene Ullman (1877–1953), heir to an ink fortune.

442–43. Mister C[octeau]. *La Phalange*, Parisian literary magazine. Arnold Bennett (1867–1931), best-selling English novelist.

444–46. The painter Charles Carolus-Duran (?1837–1917) to the painter Eugène Carrière (1849–1906), when the latter was asked by the French authorities to airbrush the pubic hair of one of his female nudes: "Are you going to shave a canvas?" Puvis de Chavannes (1824–98), French muralist.

447–50. Cf. **78.110.** Jean-Pierre Brisset, crackpot author of a work purporting to prove man's descent from the frog, elected "Prince of Thinkers" in 1913 by a group of writers including Jules Romains (1885–1972), Charles Vildrac (1882–1971), and Georges Chennevière (1884–1927) as a proto-Dadaist joke on the Parisian literary establishment.

451–53. Cf. **439** above. "My little girl" [Pound's daughter, Mary?].

462–74. London c. 1910: The Vienna (or "Wiener") Café near the British Museum, staffed by Austrian aliens ("Jozefff") and serving coffee with whipped cream ("Schlag"), shut down during WWI and later transformed into a bank; site of Pound's first meeting with Wyndham Lewis, to whom he was introduced by Laurence Binyon (1869–1943), keeper of Oriental prints and drawings at the British Museum, translator of Dante, and author of the poem "Penthesilea."

475–80. Thomas Sturge Moore (1870–1944), author of *The Rout of the Amazons* (1903), which opens "Ahi, ahi, ahi, Laomedon!" Sir Henry John Newbolt (cf. **74.277**), author of the lines "The captains passed in silence forth/And stood the door behind." Cummings, cf. **74.240.**

485–86. "It is my intention [to die] in a tavern," Goliardic drinking poem.

489–93. Robert Bridges (1844–1930), English poet laureate who commended Pound on his use of archaisms in his early poetry. Frederick James Furnivall (1825–1910), editor of the O.E.D. and founder of the Early English Text Society. Dr. Silas Weir Mitchell (1829–1914), Philadelphia editor of a Chaucer dictionary and founder of the Franklin Inn Club.

496–500. William Butler Yeats in his poem "Upon a House Shaken by the Land Agitation." Gesell, cf. **74.610.**

501. Mabel Beardsley (1872–1913), see Yeats's poem "Upon a Dying Lady."

503. From Yeats's "Reveries over Childhood and Youth" (1914), chapter 3.

504–25. During his stay in New York in 1910–11, Pound made the acquaintance of Yeats's father, the painter John Butler Yeats (1839–1922), a friend of Pound's later New York patron, the lawyer John Quinn (1870–1924). He also met the painter Warren Dahler, one of the pioneer bohemian residents of Patchin Place in Greenwich Village, where e.e. cummings (and Djuna Barnes) would later live. "Hier wohnt," here lives. 596 Lexington, address of the rooming house that was the home of Pound's maternal grandmother, Mary Weston, 1887–92. 24 E. 47th, address of the boardinghouse owned by Pound's great-uncle Ezra B. Weston and his wife Frances (Aunt Frank) Weston (cf. **74.759**). The Windsor Hotel, on 5th Avenue between 46th and 47th Streets, burned down in 1899.

526–37. The lavishly decorated home of the English painter Sir Lawrence Alma–Tadema (1836–1912) on the west side of Regent's Park, and the Moorish residence of Frederick, Lord Leighton (1830–96) on Holland Park Road. Selsey, town on the south coast of England where Ford Madox Ford ("Fordie") lived with his mistress Viola Hunt. Anecdotes referring to Swinburne's drunkenness and Tennyson's muzzy ear. Richmond, wealthy suburb of London, where Mary Elizabeth Braddon (1837–1915), author of sensationalist best-sellers, resided.

538–51. Walking tour in southern France, 1912: "Just as at Arles" (*Inf.* IX,112), Dante comparing the high walls of the cemetery of Dis to the Aliscans cemetery in Arles where warriors against the Saracens lay buried. Visiting the town of Périgueux, Pound noted that its high towers resembled New York's skyscrapers. The frescoes in the cathedral of Avignon, featuring military scenes ("and horses all armed") reminded him of the Velázquez painting at the Prado (cf. **25** above). "By Hercules! it's our township," expression of civic pride by a shoemaker in the village of Born, situated near the castle of Altafort (Hautefort), owned by the family of the troubadour poet Bertran de Born. Ventadour, site of a ruined castle associated with the troubadour Benart de Ventadorn. Aubeterre, on the river Dronne.

552–72. Cf. **74.288** and **76.289**. In 1936, Pound visited the river Piave, site of major Italian-Austrian battles in WWI, with Representative George Tinkham.

573–78. Ronald Storrs (1881–1955), English administrator and historian. "The Negus," title of Emperor Haile Selassie of Ethiopa (1891–1975), who had fled the country in 1935 after the Italian invasion. Menelik II (1844–1913), Emperor of Ethiopa, ejected the Italians in 1896.

580–81. Enrico Pea (1881–1952), Italian regionalist novelist translated by Pound. James Whitcombe Riley (1849–1916), author of American dialect poetry.

582. Nancy Cunard (cf. **74** above), who shared Pound's love for the Dordogne.

583. From Andrew Lang's translation of *Aucassin and Nicolette* (cf. **76.102**). Aucassin evokes the fair ladies in squirrel fur ("vair") and rich silk gowns ("cisclatons") whom he would gladly follow into Hell—just as Pound was briefly tempted by the affluent charms of Nancy Cunard in the 1920s?

585–86. The castle of Exicideuil, birthplace of the troubadour Giraut de Borneil, the stonework of whose parapets contains "wave patterns," here associated with the solar temple of Montségur (cf. **76.25**) and the paradisal city of Dioce (cf. **74.11**).

587. "That every month we have a new moon," from a rondeau by Froissart.

588–90. Georges Herbiet, painter and early French translator of Pound. Fritz Vanderpyl, cf. **74.369**.

592. Alfred Richard Orage (1873–1934), English editor of *The New Age*, Pound's major journalistic outlet 1913–10; Ford Madox Ford (1873–1939); René Crevel (1900–35), French Surrealist and suicide.

593. "Out of my solitude let them come," from a poem by Lope de Vega, cf. **78.201.**

594–95. Fitzgerald's *Rubáiyát*, remaindered copies of which were discovered in a bookshop by pre-Raphaelite poet and painter Dante Gabriel Rossetti (1828–82).

600–5. Cf. **75.3.** "Spewcini," i.e. Puccini. "One sees."

609–18. "Men have I know not what strange fear/. . . of beauty." Aubrey Beardsley (1872–98), English aesthete and illustrator, afflicted with tuberculosis. Sir Edward Burne-Jones (1833–98), English pre-Raphaelite painter. "Modern Beauty," by Arthur Symons (cf. **80.34**) includes the lines: "I am the torch, she saith, and what to me/If the moth die of me? I am the flame/of Beauty, and I burn that all may see."

619–21. "Brododaktulos Eôs" ("Rosy-fingered dawn"), cf. **74.658.** "Cythera deina" ("fearsome Cythera"), Aphrodite or, here, the planet Venus; cf. **596** above.

623–26. Painters of Venus: Sandro Botticelli (1444–1510), Jacopo Sellaio (1422–93), Velázquez (1599–1660), Rembrandt (1606–69), Rubens (1577–1640), Jordaens (1593–1678).

627. Chu Hsi's comments on the opening lines of the Confucian Classic, *Chung Yung* ("The Unwobbling Pivot").

630. See **169** above.

632. Sigismundo Malatesta reporting on his conversations with Platina, the papal librarian: "We talked about books, war, and men of outstanding genius."

633–42. Marie Laurencin (1885–1956), French painter. Whistler's 1872 *Arrangement in Grey Green: Miss Alexander.* John Singer Sargent (1856–1925), American society portaitist. The portrait of Belgian Symbolist poet Georges Rodenbach (1855–98), with Paris's Ile St. Louis and the Pont de la Tournelle in the background, by Lévy-Dhurmer. Elysium, the islands of the blessed. "Panta rei," everything flows.

647–48. Cf. **538** above; Aliscans derives from Alyschamps (Elysian Fields), its troughlike tombs here suggestive of the "rain-altars" among which Confucius walked (*Analects* XII, 21).

649–51. H. Spencer, Pound's instructor at the Cheltenham Military Academy, 1897–98. William Pierce Shepard, Pound's professor of Romance languages at Hamilton College, 1903–5. Siracusa, cf. **77.97.**

656–57. Cf. **79.64** for Odysseus's rash and pointless attack on the island of Ismarus; "huper moron" ("beyond what is destined"—*Od.* I, 34).

658. Zeus describing Odysseus in *Od.* I, 65–67.

659–60. "West Wind, kindly breeze." "I am at the end of my tether."

661–64. *The Pocket Book of Verse: Great English and American Poems*, edited by M.E. Speare, Ph.D. (New York, 1940), discovered in the latrine, contained 18 pages of Whitman as well as Richard Lovelace's "To Althea, from Prison," and selections from the King James version of the Bible, including the Book of Job, chapter 38: "Have the gates of death been revealed unto thee?/Or hast thou seen the gates of the shadow of death?"

665–67. Cf. *Od.* V, 365ff., where Odysseus's raft is destroyed by a storm created by Poseidon and he is saved from drowning by Ino, daughter of Cadmus, transformed into Leucothea. The "air strip" refers to the steel mats (used to construct temporary airplane runways) which were installed to reinforce the cage in which Odysseus-Pound spent his first three weeks at Pisa before his "raft broke" and he was transferred to a tent in the medical compound.

668–71. From the *Catholic Prayer Book*: "Immaculate," "I shall go [unto the altar of God]" (preparation for mass). Three martyred saints recalled in the "Memento for the Dead" prayer; their names mean "Eternal, "Good," and "Reborn." "Per omnia saecula saeculorum" ("world without end"), from the Latin mass.

672–75. Echoes the liturgical "Repos eternel donne a cil" ("Grant him eternal rest") from the "Epitaphe et Rondeau" of Villon's *Testament*. Pound's French, however, literally translates: "give rest to eyelashes." "It acts without end," from Pound's Italian translation of the *Chung Yung*, which in English reads: "The unmixed functions without bourne. This unmixed is the tensile light, the Immaculata. There is no end to its action." During his first three weeks at Pisa, there was indeed no end to the light's action, for in his "death cell" Pound was exposed to the sun all day and to electric reflector lamps all night, causing considerable eye problems. "The tears I have created flood me/Late, very late, have I known you, Sadness" (cf. Saint Augustine, *Confessions* X, 27, "Sero ti amavi": "Late have I loved you, Beauty so old and so new! Late have I loved you!").

682–83. "Yesterday." For the Elpenor tag, cf. **74.495**.

686–87. "With thanks to." The black trainee Wiseman ("from Africa"), as opposed to William Wiseman, ex-head of British Intelligence and international financier with the New York firm of Kuhn, Loeb & Company.

689. "The underground." The manuscript drafts of Canto 74 speak even more explicitly of an initiatory descent into the labyrinth: "you are come into mind/in the labyrinth & I cd not save you/nor find you a thread of issue."

690–92. Mark Alfred Carlton (1886–1925), American agronomist who developed new and hardier strains of wheat, oat, and barley, here associated with Demeter, goddess of grain.

699. Cf. **74.495** and **76.224**.

704. "O[f] t[he] a[rmy]?"

705. Imitation of Browning's "Home-Thoughts from Abroad" (in Speare's *Pocket Book of Verse*): "Oh, to be in England/Now that April's there."

714–17. The tower attic at Lacock Abbey in Salisbury Plain containing a copy of the 1225 Magna Carta, which "confirmed" the 1100 Charter presented to King John by his barons.

723. Gilbert Keith Chesteron (1874–1936), Catholic writer and eminent Edwardian.

729. Charles Talbot, cousin of Pound's wife Dorothy, inheritor of Lacock Abbey. The Talbot's family emblem included a dog.

733. From John Still (1543–1608), "Jolly Good Ale and Old," in Speare.

740. Posh London hotel.

741–49. Hewlitt (cf. **74.276**) lived in Salisbury, where Pound visited him on Christmas Eve, 1911. "Heigh ho! sing, heigh ho! unto the green holly," from Shakespeare's *As You Like It*, in Speare.

750. Lady Anne Blunt, wife of W.S. Blunt (cf. **81.169**), née Anne Isabella King-Noël.

751–53. French fishing port associated by Pound with Swinburne (cf. **82.21**), author of a play dealing with Mary Stuart ("la Stuarda"), who was also the subject of a novel, *The Queen's Quair* (1903), by Maurice Hewlett.

754. "If all the griefs and laments and pain," from Bertran de Born's funeral lament for the young king Henry (cf. **84.2**).

756–67. Tudor, the royal family that ruled England from the beginning of Henry VII's reign in 1485 to the death of Elizabeth in 1603. The War of the Roses opposed the House of York (White) and the House of Lancaster (Red). Catharine Howard (?1521–42), fifth wife of Henry VIII, beheaded for her immoral conduct. Anne Boleyn (?1507–36), second wife of Henry VIII and mother of Queen Elizabeth, also beheaded. The three stanzas imitate the strophic forms of Fitzgerald's *Rubáiyát of Omar Khayyám*, anthologized in Speare.

770. A curved pond in Hyde Park, near Pound's prewar lodgings in Kensington.

CANTO 81

1–3. Demeter, goddess of the harvest; Cythera, the planet Venus.

4–17. "Here is much Catholicism/ . . . and very little religion/ . . . I believe that kings will disappear." Padre José, cf. **77.83**. "Eat bread," cf. **80.15**. Velázquez, cf. **80.25**.

22–35. Claude Gernade Bowers, American ambassador to Spain, 1933–39. Francisco Franco (1892–1975), Spanish dictator. Alcázar, town visited by Pound in 1906. "That is mourning, Ha!/my husband is dead." "Locanda," inn.

38–47. Basil Bunting (cf. **74.230**) remembering local customs in the Canary Islands; T.S. Eliot (cf. **74.9**) on Portuguese folk dances in his summer home in Gloucester, Mass.; Horace Cole (cf. **80.320**) mounting a street demonstration in Soho when Italy entered WWI.

48–54. The French *vers libriste* André Spire (cf. **77.236**) bemoaning corruption on the agricultural credit board. Ex-President John Adams writing his friend ex-President Thomas Jefferson, "You are apprehensive of monarchy, I, of aristocracy" (Canto 69).

56–58. Josef Bard (1882–1975), Hungarian writer. François, duc de La Rochefoucauld (1613–80), celebrated for his maxims. Marquise de Maintenon (1635–1719), second wife of Louis XIV, known for her wit.

59–62. "I'll tear out your guts"/"And I'll pluck yours out too." Threats exchanged between Sigismundo Malatesta and Frederigo d'Urbino (Canto 10). Mencken, cf. **79.93**.

63–64. Dorothy Pound's conjugal agreement stipulated that she not be required to cook; hence a lifetime of restaurants.

65. "Iunx . . . emon poti dôma ton andra," ("Little wheel . . . man to my house"), from Theocritus, *Idylls* 2: a magic spell uttered by a young maid sixteen times to draw her errant lover back to her house.

67–70. The Frobenius Institute in Frankfurt housed various masks from Benin (in southern Nigeria) collected by the German anthropologist. Cf. **74.319**.

76–80. Santayana (cf. **74.304**), born in Madrid, came to the United States in 1872. Mussolini was born in the region of Romagna.

84–93. George Horace Lorimer (1868–1937), editor-in-chief of the *Saturday Evening Post* and a neighbor of the Pounds in the Philadelphia surburb of Wyncote, managing to extract articles from Senator Albert Beveridge (1862–1927) about his 1899 inspection trip to the Philippines.

94. In Pound's 1916 translation of the Noh play *Kinuta*, this cry of grief is uttered first by the wife (and then by her ghost and by the chorus) when she realizes she has been abandoned by her husband.

96. From Richard Lovelace's "To Althea, from Prison" ("When Love with unconfinèd wings/Hovers within my gates,/And my divine Althea brings/To whisper at the grates"), in Speare.

101–2. Henry Lawes (1596–1662), English composer who set Waller's poem "Go, lovely Rose" (in Speare). John Jenkins (1592–1678), English composer and musician. Dolmetsch, cf. **80.391.**

108. Cf. **74.839.**

113. Edmund Waller (1606–87), cf. **100** above; John Dowland (1563–1626), Irish composer and lutanist.

114–16. From Chaucer's "Merciless Beaute," a triple roundel thought to be composed around 1380, thus roughly 180 years before Shakespeare's birth.

117. "And listening to the gentle murmur," perhaps a trace of Pound's Italian Cantos of Jan.-Feb. 1945. Cf. the visionary encounters with the three female apparitions ("tre donne") at **76.11–31** and **78.210**

119. For "hypostasis," cf. **76.182.**

120–21. In one of the drafts of Italian Cantos 74–75, Pound-Basinio's glimpse of Cunizza on the hillside near Sant'Ambrogio modulates into a larger vision of a theatrical troupe whose women are dressed for carnival (cf. the "half-mask's space" below).

124. From the Greek, "set apart," or displaced (as opposed to "hypostasis," i.e. "set beneath," as of a foundation or base?). Can also refer to the dilation of the pupils, as in "Hugh Selwyn Mauberley" ("inconscient, full gaze,/The wide-banded irides/And botticellian sprays implied/in their diastasis").

127. "Eidôs," participial form of the Greek verb for knowing or seeing. Cf. **76.180,** "nor is this yet *atasal.*"

130–33. Three pairs of eyes of different colors?

134. A pointed reply, on one level, to the famous axiom of Oscar Wilde's prison poem, "The Ballad of Reading Gaol" (in Speare): "And all men kill the thing they love."

139. After this line, an earlier typescript version of this Canto moved into the following passage, subsequently canceled: "So thinking of Althea at the grates/Two rose-like lips pressed down upon my own//for the full eidos the form to/pass and intercross//each space full of its formed life/that moves and keeps defined/its clarity its demarkation/ what thou lovest remains/the rest is dross."

145. "Vanity of vanities, saith the Preacher; all is vanity," from *Ecclesiastes* (in Speare).

151. Jeanne Paquin (1869–1936), French dress designer, known as the queen of Paris fashion at the turn of the century. Cf. **74.364** and **80.778.**

153. Refracts a line from Chaucer's "Ballade of Good Counsel" ("Subdue thyself, and others thee shall hear"), modernized by Henry Van Dyke, in Speare.

155–56. Cf. Pound's musical setting of "L'Epitaphe de Villon" ("Ballade des Pendus"): "La pluie nous a bués et lavés./Et le soleil desséchés et noircis;/Pies, corbeaux, nous ont les yeux cavés,/Et arrachée la barbe et les sourcils." ("The rain has washed and cleansed us/And the sun dried and blackened us,/Magpies and crows have pecked out our eyes/And plucked off our beards and brows.")

169. Pound's memory of Wilfred Scawen Blunt (1840–1922) was perhaps jogged by his double sonnet, "With Esther," included in Speare (and containing the lines "Till I too learn'd what dole of vanity/Will serve a human soul for daily bread"). A poet and political activist, jailed by the British for two months in Ireland as a political prisoner, Blunt was the author of *Shame of the 19th Century* (1900), a scathing indictment of British imperialism, hence perhaps his "unconquered flame." In January 1914, Pound organized a visit of six poets (including Yeats and Sturge Moore) to Blunt's country estate in Essex, where they presented him with a Gaudier-Breszka sculpture in his honor.

CANTO 82

1. Orion and the dog star Sirius.

2. "Good morning, sir."

7–22. Algernon Charles Swinburne (1837–1909) was still alive when Pound arrived in England in 1908, but he never managed to meet him. Walter Savage Landor (1775–1864), English writer, author of the poem "Dirce" (cf. **76.9**), whom the young Swinburne visited in the last year of his life. Elkin Matthews (1851–1921), London publisher of Pound's early works. Theodore Watts-Duncan (1832–1914), caretaker of Swinburne in his dotage. In his biography of Swinburne, Edmond Gosse tells the anecdote of Swinburne of being plucked from the English Channel by French fishermen at Yport; once safe, the English poet proceeded to recite the republican verse of Victor Hugo (and not Aeschylus) to his rescuers.

23–27. From the opening scene of Aeschylus's *Agamemnon* (translated by Pound into demotic African-American but never published, *c.* 1919): the watchman lies awake on the roof ("like a dog"), observing the procession of the stars at night. "EMOS POSIS . . . CHEROS," ("my husband [dead by this right] hand"), Clytaemnestra boasting of her murder of Agamemnon, in the original Greek and Latin translation.

28–30. The doughty Blunt (cf. **81.169**) essaying his skill as a matador in Madrid in 1862, suggesting the adventure stories of Canadian novelist Frank Packard (1877–1942) and the foreign exploits of Percy Bysshe Shelley (1792–1822).

31–32. Basinio Basini, cf. **74.445**, Malatesta's court poet and Poundian alter ego who wrote 30 epistles celebrating Sigismundo's love for Isotta and inscribed Greek tags (or rhythmic "moulds") in the margins of his Latin compositions to keep his melodic sense active.

33–34. James Otis, author of one of the first American Greek grammars (cf. **78.189**). Hieronymos Soncino (?1460–1534), Renaissance printer who introduced books printed in Hebrew and Greek. "Marble," a printer's imposing-stone.

36–41. The English printers of Clowes and Sons, Ltd., objected to 25 poems in Pound's 1916 volume *Lustra* as obscene, and the book was brought out by publisher Elkin Matthews in an expurgated version. The English essayist Augustine Birrell (1850–1933) compared Pound's brush with censorship to that of the Irish poet Thomas Moore (1770–1852) and English poet Samuel Rogers (1763–1855).

48. Cf. **80.501**.

49–51. John Masefield (1878–1967), English poet. Yeats's friend Sturge Moore (cf. **80. 476**).

52–65. Stanislawa Tomczyk, Polish medium whose feats of telekinesis fascinated Yeats, a member of the Society of Psychical Research and resident of 18 Woburn Buildings in London. Francis Tancred, an early Imagist poet, to whom Pound facetiously ascribes a Crusader ancestry.

67. "Objects, not words."

70. Ideogram: *jên²*, "humaneness" (man balanced between heaven and earth).

72. From Landor's "Dirce" (cf. **16** above): "Stand close around, ye Stygian set,/With Dirce in one boat conveyed!/Or Charon, seeing may forget/That he is old and she a shade."

73. Pastiche of Robert Burn's "To a Mouse" (in Speare).

81. Cf. **78.19.**

82–83. Cf. **78.222.**

91–92. The watchman on the roof at the opening of the *Agamemnon* awaiting the signals of the beacon fires (cf. **23** above).

93–98. Richard Riethmuller, author of *Walt Whitman and the Germans* (1906) and Pound's instructor of German at the University of Pennsylvania (just across the river from Camden, N.J., Whitman's birthplace). The Whitman lines are drawn from "Out of the Cradle Endlessly Rocking," in Speare.

99. "Earth," in Greek and Latin.

109–10. "Was Nicolo [buried]/and [having fathered sons] on this side and the other of the Po." Niccolò d'Este (1384–1441), ruler of Ferrara, requested that he be buried simply, with no clothes on, in order to rejoin the earth (Canto 24).

111. Cf. **81.65.**

115. Cf. **77.103.**

118–25. "The marriage of the earth . . .mystery." "She said my husband," from the *Agamemnon*, cf. **25** above. "CHTHONIOS" ("earth-born"), "CHTHONOS" ("of the earth (or netherworld)"). "ICHOR," the fluid that flows in the veins of the gods.

129–30. "Dakruôn," ("crying" or "of tears"). "Enteuthen" ("whereupon").

CANTO 83

1–2. "Hudor" ("water"). "Peace."

3–4. Gemistus Plethon (?1355–?1450), Byzantine Neoplatonist who considered Poseidon, the god of sea, the greatest of the divinities. Sigismundo Malatesta had his ashes removed to the Tempio at Rimini, whose bas-reliefs feature aquatic motifs.

7–21. "For light/is an attribute of fire," tag from Scotus Erigena (cf. **74.155** for Erigena and King Carolus or "Charles the Bald"). C.B. Schlüter, the "priest" who edited Erigina's *De Divisione Naturae* (1818), underscored the philosopher's "piety and cheerfulness" (*hilaritas*). "Always Paris." "Pyx," a casket of precious metal to hold the Host. "Omnia, quae sunt," cf. **74.139.** For Erigena exhumed and Simon de Monfort, cf. **74.158.**

22. Cf. **74.457.**

23–26. W.B. Yeats at the Notre Dame Cathedral in Paris in 1922, perhaps noting the statue of Mother and Child haloed by a rose window—or perhaps simply missing the forest through the trees.

27–28. Romanesque church in Toulouse; Santa Maria Dei Miracoli, in Venice, cf. **76.271.**

35–37. *Analects* VI, 21.

38–39. From Yeats's "Down by Sally Gardens" ("She bid me take life easy, as the grass grows on the weirs;/But I was young and foolish, and now am full of tears"). "Consiros" ("with grief or longing [I look upon my past folly]"), Arnaut Daniel's Provençal in *Pur.* XXVI, 144.

40–53. "Dog and Cat," a meeting of streets near Siena's San Giorgio cathedral. The traditional procession with wax offerings to the Madonna is held at the church on the eve of the Palio. "Should your love be." Cf. **80.128.** "Olim," cf. **76.311.** "Maria's face," cf. **74.745.** Further family resemblances suggested by Thomas Hardy's poem "The Family Face."

54–58. "Panta rei," cf. **80.641–48.** *Mencius* IV, 2, xviii, reporting Confucius's praise of water.

60. A reminiscence of Rilke's 1907 poem, "The Panther"?

64. "Dryas," tree nymph. "Dryad" was Pound's name for his first love, the poet Hilda Doolittle ("H.D."), whose September 10th birthday this passage may celebrate.

81. "More things diaphanous," from *De Luce*, the treatise on light by the medieval philosopher Robert Grosseteste (?1175–1253), crucial to Pound's Cavalcanti.

90–102. Paraphrase of Mencius II, 2, xiiiff.

108. "Don't fight."

111–14. Ideograms: *wu⁴ chu⁴ ch'ang³*, "not help grow." From Mencius II, 2, xvi ("Kung-Sun Chow"), a parable about a farmer who, attempting to make his corn grow taller, pulled it up by the roots.

115–25. San Gregorio, San Trovaso, San Vio, churches in Venice. "Ziovan," Venetian pronunciation of Giovan[nni]. "Redentore," annual summer boat festival. "Le Zattere" ("the rafts"), long embankment on the northern edge of the Giudecca Canal. "Ca[sa]," house in Venetian dialect. "Ca' Foscari, Ca' Giustinian," palazzi on the Grand Canal. "Sensaria" ("Brokerage House").

129–30. "The wasp." I.e. Braceliande, the enchanted forest of Arthurian romance?

141. Trainees assigned to weeding the grass at the DTC by Lt. Jones, provost officer of the camp.

152. "Eis chthonious" ("to those beneath the earth"), here the Underworld of Persephone and Tiresias.

156. "Christ the King, God the Sun."

159. Cf. the Paolo and Francesca episode of *Inf.* V, 138: "quel giorno più non vi leggemmo avante" ("that day we read no farther in it").

160. Cf. Swinburne's "A Forsaken Garden" (in Speare): "What love was ever as deep as a grave?"

161. "Painted scroll."

163–92. Pound spent the winters of 1913 through 1915 serving as Yeats's secretary at the latter's country home, Stone Cottage, in Coleman's Hatch, Sussex. Near the coast, the area was considered a "prohibited area" by British military authorities during WWI, and Pound and his wife were accordingly served a summons (later withdrawn) for their illegal presence there. Among the works Pound read aloud to Yeats (whose eyes were weak): seven volumes of Wordsworth, *The History of Magic* (1854), by Joseph Ennemoser, and Charles Doughty's epic poem, *The Dawn in Britain* (1906). Yeats's 1914 poem "The Peacock," memorializing the roast peacock dinner Blunt had offered Yeats and Pound on the occasion of their January 1914 visit (cf. **81.169**) runs, "What's riches to him/That has made a great peacock/With the pride of his eye?" "Aere perennius," ([a work of art] "more enduring than bronze"), Horace, *Odes*, III. xxx.1.

197–202 Cf. the (three) pairs of eyes at **81.133–34.** Recalls the particular mechanism of the "spirits" in Cavalcanti's poetry, which, passing through the eyes, are violently directed by the Lady's gaze into the lover's heart, where, inscribed like a scar, they in turn illuminate his vision of Love. Cf. Pound's 1912 translation of "Ballata VII"—"She said, 'That lady, who upon thine heart/Cut her full image, clear, by Love's device,/Hath looked so fixedly in through thine eyes/That she's made Love appear there.'"

205–17. "And/they say to me/the ladies/you are an old man/Anacreon" (tag, in German, from the *Anacreontea*). A "15th-century Madonna" realized as a "20th-century

Madonna" in Bacher's Tyrolian wood carvings (cf. **74.819**). "That is called Walter Square," in the South Tyrolian town of Bozen/Bolzano, named after the medieval German minnesinger Walther von der Vogelweide.

224. I.e. the House of Parliament.

226. Ninian Edwards (1775–1833), U.S. senator from Illinois.

235. From the English folk song, "The Keeper" ("Hey down, ho down,/Derry derry down/Among the leaves so green O").

CANTO 84

1–5. Pound received a letter from his wife, Dorothy, on October 8, informing him of the death of John Penrose Angold (1909–43) while on active service in the RAF. Pound greatly admired both his poetry and his writings on economics, some of which he planned to translate into Italian. "Angold tethneke" ("Angold is dead"). Provençal from Bernart de Born's lament for the young king (cf. **80.754**). In one of the typescripts, this canto's opening threnody was preceded by the following valediction, apparently composed in anticipation of imminent death: "Yet from my tomb such flame of love arise/that whoso passes shall be warmed thereby;/let stray cats curl there/where no tomb stone is/and girls' eyes sparkle at the unmarked spot/Let rancours die/and a slow drowse of peace pervade who passes."

6–14. John Hollis Bankhead, senator from Alabama (1930–46), referring to President Roosevelt. William Edgar Borah, senator from Idaho (1907–40). Pound met with both of them during his 1939 visit to Washington D.C., where he hoped to influence U.S. economic policy and avert the coming war.

15–17. Pastiche of Blake or Burns (in Speare)?

18. Captain in charge of prisoner training at the DTC.

24–25. Henry Crowder, African-American jazz musician, Nancy Cunard's lover and moving force behind her *Negro: An Anthology* (1934), here phantasmatically associated with the black trainees. Slaughter, a major at the DTC.

26–31. *Time* magazine, October 1: At an isolationist rally in Chicago, the nonagenarian political activist Jacob Coxley (1854–1951) criticized the interest the government paid on privately issued bonds. The same issue featured the story "A Rope for Haw-Haw," reporting that the radio broadcaster William Joyce (with whom Pound had corresponded during the '40s) had been found guilty of treason and sentenced "to be hanged by the neck until dead." *Time*, October 8: cover story on Sinclair Lewis (1885–1953), with a review of his latest work, *Cass Timberlane*, and a brief obituary of Hungarian composer Bela Bartók (1881–1945). The same issue contained a photo of corpses stacked in a mass grave at Belsen and an account of the trial by British authorities in Lünenburg of 45 men and women who had worked at the concentration camps of Belsen and Oswiecim [i.e. Auschwitz].

32. Charles Beard (1874–1938), American historian and author of the Armed Services Edition of *The Republic: Conversations on Fundamentals* (1943), a commentary on the U.S. Constitution.

35. Pound identified with President John Adams's opposition to U.S. involvement in foreign wars and his distrust of banks of discount (Cantos 70–71).

41–46. From Dorothy's letters to Pound. September 28: "I have burnt incense to Apollo several times for help." October 5 (recounting her return to Rapallo after having visited him at the DTC on October 3): "Carrara *splendid*—it snowed the night I was in Massa & the tops were snow-white, next a.m., as against stone-white—a real relief to see anything so lovely."

47–49. Memories of travels in the Pyrennees in the summer of 1919 with Dorothy.

50–55. T'ao Chi'en (365–427), Chinese poet who retired from public life; his "Peach-blossom fountain" nostalgically evokes the lost paradise of his youth in the "old Dynasty." Ho Ci'u, town in Shansi Province. "Cythera deina" ("fearsome Cythera").

56–62. George C. Carson, a friend of the Pound's parents, *c.* 1910.

63–67. Cf. **74.759** and **74.783.**

68–69. A quip by Natalie Barney (cf. **80.411**) about having gotten a great deal out of life, "perhaps more than was in it."

70. "Sky of Pisa."

74–76. The reign of Cheou-sin, last emperor of the Yin dynastasy (12th century B.C.) was so cruel and corrupt that "the Viscount of Wei retired, the Vicount of Chi became a slave, and Pikan protested and died." *Analects* XVII, 16. "Jên²," cf. **82.70.**

77–80. "Xaire" ("Hail"). Alessandro Pavolini and Fernando Mezzasoma, senior officials of the Salò Republic, the former the secretary of the Fascist Republican Party and the latter the minister of popular culture. Pound corresponded at length with both in 1943–45; both were shot by partisans at Dongo and subsequently hung by their heels with "il Capo" ("the Boss") in Milan on April 29, 1945 (cf. **74.4**). Pierre Laval (cf. **76.245**), executed for treason, October 15, 1945. Vidkun Quisling (cf. **80.44**), executed for treason, October 24, 1945. Phillipe Henriot, French journalist and radio broadcaster, minister of propaganda for the Vichy government, shot by the French Resistance, June 28, 1944.

82–86. William Bullitt (1891–1967) divested himself of his stocks before the Depression and went into government as ambassador to the USSR and France (1936–41). Dorothy Pound sold the Imperial Chemicals, Ltd. stocks she had inherited so as not to profit from "blood money."

87. "When you come to the summit of the stair," slightly misquoted from Arnaut Daniel's speech (in Provençal) in *Pur.* XXVI, 142–147. Translated by Pound in 1910 as: "Arnaut am I who weep and go a-singing./In thought I see my folly of old days,/Yet see, rejoicing, the day which is before me,/for which I hope and now pray you in that power's name,/Which guideth you unto the summit of the stair,/Be mindful of my grief in good time."

88. "Ethos" ("custom, usage, character").

90. Ideogram: *ming²*, translated by Pound as "the sun and moon, the total light process . . . hence the intelligence."

91. See the Adams Cantos (62–71).

93. Cf. **77.12.**

96–97. Cf. **74.340.**

98–104. Winston Churchill was defeated in the election of July 26, 1945. "Kumrad Koba," i.e. Stalin (cf. **74.711**), quoted in *Time* magazine, August 27, 1945. "Winston, P.M." deleted in the 1949 Faber edition.

105–12. "And then I said to the sister/of the little swinekeeper:/and these Americans? do they behave well?/and she: not very./Not very well at all./And I: worse than the Germans?/and she: the same." The Faber printing adds the Greek phrase "dia uphorba" (divine swineherdess) at the end of line 110.

113. Joseph Lincoln Steffens (1866–1939) deeply impressed Pound in the early '20s with his first-hand accounts of the Russian Revolution.

116. Arthur Hendrick Vandenberg (1884–1952), U.S. delegate to the United Nations conference in San Francisco, 1945. Cf. **74.43** for Pound's belief that if he could only learn Georgian, he might be able to convert Stalin to his economic doctrines.

118–19. In a letter of September 28, Dorothy wrote that she was reading the "very ideogrammatic" sonnets of Shakespeare. The rhymes here probably echo the final couplet of Sonnet 107 (included in Speare and in Pound's own 1964 anthology, *Confucius to Cummings*): "And thou in this shalt find thy monument,/When tyrants' crest and tombs of brass are spent." In one of the typescripts of this canto, the closing couplet was followed by the lines, subsequently canceled, "Italy, my Italy, my God, my Italy/Ti abbraccio la terra santa" ("I embrace you the holy land").

SELECTED POEMS
AVAILABLE FROM NEW DIRECTIONS

Eugénio de Andrade ▪ *Homero Aridjis* ▪ *Charles Baudelaire*

Gottfried Benn* ▪ Johannes Bobrowski ▪ William Bronk

René Char ▪ Cid Corman ▪ H.D. (Hilda Doolittle)

Robert Duncan ▪ Gavin Ewart ▪ Hans Faverey

Lawrence Ferlinghetti ▪ Allen Grossman ▪ *Eugène Guillevic*

Lars Gustafsson ▪ Samuel Hazo ▪ *Vicente Huidobro*

James Laughlin ▪ Irving Layton ▪ Denise Levertov

Li Po ▪ Luljeta Lleshanaku ▪ *Federico García Lorca*

Hugh MacDiarmid ▪ Stephane Mallarmé

Thomas Merton ▪ *Henri Michaux** ▪ *Eugenio Montale*

Charles Olson* ▪ Toby Olson ▪ José Emilio Pacheco

Michael Palmer ▪ *Nicanor Parra* ▪ Boris Pasternak*

Kenneth Patchen ▪ Octavio Paz ▪ *Saint-John Perse*

Po Chü-I ▪ Ezra Pound ▪ Kenneth Rexroth

Rainer Maria Rilke ▪ Jerome Rothenberg

Delmore Schwartz ▪ Peter Dale Scott ▪ C.H. Sisson

Stevie Smith ▪ Gary Snyder* ▪ *Jules Supervielle**

Dylan Thomas ▪ Charles Tomlinson ▪ Tu Fu

Paul Valéry* ▪ Vernon Watkins ▪ Jonathan Williams

William Carlos Williams

Authors in italics = bilingual editions
Authors with an asterisk = poetry with prose

please visit our website
www.ndpublishing.com
or order from you local bookstore